Life in the UK Test
Practice Questions

**Questions and answers for the
British citizenship test**

....

Published by Red Squirrel Publishing

Red Squirrel Publishing
Suite 235, 77 Beak Street,
London W1F 9DB, United Kingdom

www.redsquirrelbooks.com

First edition published in 2006
Third edition – First impression

ISBN: 978-0-9552-1599-5

Edited by Henry Dillon and George Sandison

Designed and artworked by
Cox Design Limited, Witney, Oxon

Printed in Czechoslovakia by Finidr

CONTENTS

INTRODUCTION

The Life in the UK test is an essential part of the process for anyone planning on becoming a British citizen or applying for Indefinite Leave to Remain. Passing the test is compulsory under the 'Knowledge of life and language in the UK' requirement of your application.

Before October 2013, if you have passed the Life in the UK test you meet the knowledge of life and language requirement. However, if you make your application on or after 28 October 2013 you will be required to both pass the Life in the UK test and also have a speaking and listening qualification in English at B1 Common European Framework of Reference for Languages (CEFR) or higher, or its equivalent. Exceptions are made for applicants from majority English-speaking countries.

Over 150,000 people take the Life in the UK Test every year but not all of them pass. With each attempt costing £50, this can be an expensive and timely mistake. However, with the right preparation, you can be one of those who passes first time.

About this book

This book is designed to test your knowledge and understanding of the official study materials. This introduction offers advice on how to prepare for the test and guidance on the kinds of question you will face in your test.

There are 20 complete practice tests, each containing 24 questions in the same format as the actual test. The questions are all based on the testable sections of the official study materials, and these are the following chapters:

- The values and principles of the UK
- What is the UK?
- A long and illustrious history
- A modern, thriving society
- The UK government, the law and your role.

You should read all of this introduction before you take any practice tests to help you prepare and understand all of the features of this book.

Take some time to read through the following sections carefully. They tell you about all the features of this book and will enable you to get as much out of it as possible.

How to prepare for the test

1. Study the materials

The first and most important step of your preparations is to study the complete official study materials. These are found in the Home Office handbook, *Life in the United Kingdom: A Guide for New Residents* and are reproduced in our titles, *Life in the UK Test: Study Guide & Handbook*. You can find more information about these books at **www.lifeintheuk.net/studyguide**

It is essential that you read and understand the testable chapters before taking your test. Taking practice tests alone will not prepare you for the real test.

2. Take practice tests

Once you've finished thoroughly reviewing the study materials, you should check if you are ready to take the test by completing several practice tests from this book.

When you sit your official test you will be given 45 minutes to complete the test. So when you take a practice test you should allow yourself the same time. The pass mark in the official test is at least 75% – or only six incorrect answers. Again, this is what you should aim to score when you take a practice test.

If you can consistently score at least 75% and finish a test within 45 minutes, then you are ready to take your official test.

If you do not pass the practice tests satisfactorily and do not feel confident enough to sit your official test, then you should continue your study of the testable materials. If you do not have sufficient time left before your official test to do more study, then you may be able to reschedule your test appointment. You can reschedule your test without charge up to seven days before the date. If you cancel your booking with less than seven days' notice your booking fee will not be refunded.

3. Online tests

Once you've finished testing yourself using the questions in this book, you can go online and access further tests with our free subscription offer.

Visit **www.lifeintheuk.net/test** and register an account to redeem this offer.

WARNING: DO NOT MEMORISE QUESTIONS

The practice questions contained in this book are intended to help you assess your understanding of the study materials and check if you are ready to take the official test.

Do not prepare for the test by memorising the questions in this book.

All the questions are in the same format as the official test questions. But they are not identical to the questions in the official test. The Home Office regularly revises the wording of questions used in the Life in the UK Test.

It is very important that you fully read and understand the study materials before taking your test.

SEND US YOUR FEEDBACK

Our books have helped thousands of people pass the Life in the UK Test. So we're always delighted when we hear from our readers. You can send us your comments by visiting **www.lifeintheuk.net/feedback**

CHECKLIST

There are a lot of things that you need to remember to do for the Life in the UK Test. Avoid problems and get organised by completing this checklist.

☐ Test appointment booked

Book your test through the UKBA website **www.lituktestbooking.co.uk** or by calling the Life in the UK Test Helpline on **0800 015 4245**

Test Date .... Time ....

Test Centre Address ....

....

....

Phone ....

☐ Finished reading study materials

☐ Completed all practice tests in this book

☐ Completed free online practice tests at **www.lifeintheuk.net**

☐ Checked latest tips and advice at **www.lifeintheuk.net**

☐ Checked your registered details exactly match your photo ID

☐ Checked your proof of address is valid

☐ Confirmed test centre location and travel route

QUESTIONS TO EXPECT

All questions in the Life in the UK Test are multiple-choice. There are four different formats in which a question may be asked:

1. **One correct answer – Choose the correct answer to the question from four options**

   ## EXAMPLE
   What important event in the development of women's rights happened in 1928?

   - **A** Women were first given the right to vote.
   - **B** Women were given the right to vote at the same age as men.
   - **C** The first divorce laws were introduced.
   - **D** Women were allowed to keep their own earnings and property.

2. **Two correct answers – Choose two correct answers to the question from four options**

   ## EXAMPLE
   Which TWO of the following are famous Paralympians?

   - **A** Baroness Tanni Grey-Thompson
   - **B** Dame Kelly Holmes
   - **C** Jayne Torvill
   - **D** Ellie Simmonds

3. **True or False – Decide whether a statement is true or false**

   ## EXAMPLE
   Is the statement below TRUE or FALSE?
   A newspaper's owner may try to influence government policy by running a campaign

   - **A** True
   - **B** False

4. Select correct statement – Choose the correct statement from two options

EXAMPLE

Which of these statements is correct?

 A Florence Nightingale is often regarded as the founder of modern nursing.

B Florence Nightingale pioneered the use of syringes in hospitals.

Working through the answers

When you start your test, make sure you read each question carefully. Make sure you understand it.

If you are confident that you know the correct answer, make your selection and move on to the next question.

It is vital that you select an answer for every question even if you are not confident that it is correct. There is a chance that even a guess will be correct! If you do this, make sure that you note the question number on your blank paper. It is possible that a question later in the test will help you to answer a question that you have found difficult.

Traps to watch out for

Some questions may be worded so that an option may be a TRUE statement but not be the CORRECT answer to the question being asked.

Be careful if questions and answers use words that are absolute. These words mean that the question or answer applies in all cases (e.g. *always*, *every*) or not at all (e.g. *never*).

EXAMPLE

Which of the following statements is correct?

A There are a few members of Parliament who do not represent any of the main political parties.

B All members of Parliament have to belong to a political party.

The second statement is absolute. There are no exceptions. This means the correct answer is A because, whether or not there are currently independent MPs in Parliament, there *can* be independent MPs in Parliament.

You also need to be careful of words that *moderate* a question or answer. When words such as *often, rarely, sometimes* and *usually* are used, this means that the question or answer is referring to something that is not true in all cases.

EXAMPLE

Who usually chooses who will be the Archbishop of Canterbury?

- **A** The monarch
- **B** The Prime Minister and a committee appointed by the Church
- **C** A committee appointed by the Church
- **D** The Prime Minister

In the above example, all of the options could be correct. The monarch has the right to choose, but does not in practice. Whilst both a committee appointed by the Church and the Prime Minister are both usually involved in the decision. This means that C and D are accurate, but not correct because they don't provide a full answer. B is the only answer that fully answers the question.

Also watch for negative words in questions or answers – such as *not, never* and *neither*. These words can be easily overlooked and completely change the meaning of the question being asked.

EXAMPLE

Which of these socially progressive measures was not introduced during the early years of the 20th century?

- **A** Free school meals
- **B** Old-age pensions
- **C** Financial help for the unemployed
- **D** Equal pay for women

In the example above, notice that the question is asking for the statement that is not correct. Free school meals, old-age pensions and financial help for the unemployed were all introduced at the start of the 20th century. There are no laws enforcing equal pay conditions for women in the UK, however. Therefore, although option D is a false statement, it is the correct answer for this question.

For some questions, one of the answers may read: 'All of the above'. In these cases, read the other answers carefully to see if it is possible that they are all correct. Even if two of the three answers seem correct, all three alternative answers must be correct for you to choose the 'all of the above' option.

For some questions, one of the answers may read: 'None of the above'. In these cases, read the other answers carefully to see if it is possible that they are all incorrect. Even if two of the three answers seem incorrect, all three alternative answers must be wrong for you to choose the 'none of the above' option.

PRACTICE TEST 1

1   **Who did Henry VIII marry after the execution of Anne Boleyn?**

   A Catherine Howard

   B Catherine Parr

   C Anne of Cleves

   D Jane Seymour

2   **How old was Edward VI when he died?**

   A 15

   B 18

   C 56

   D 35

3   **Scotland changed in which TWO ways after the Battle of Culloden?**

   A Chieftains became landlords if they had the favour of the English king

   B Chieftains took control of the land away from the English king

   C Clansmen became tenants who had to pay for the land they used

   D The clans were entirely destroyed

4   **The Battle of the Boyne is celebrated with a bank holiday in which country?**

   A England

   B Wales

   C Northern Ireland

   D Scotland

5   Which TWO of these statements are true?

   A Snowdonia is a national park.

   B The Tower of London is not open to the public.

   C The Lake District is England's largest national park.

   D Elizabeth Tower was named after Queen Elizabeth I.

6   The Union Flag symbolises the union between which countries?

   A England, Wales, Scotland and Ireland

   B England, Wales and Scotland

   C England, Wales and Ireland

   D England and the American colonies

7   Which of these people could be regarded as the greatest playwright of all time?

   A Sir Francis Drake

   B Geoffrey Chaucer

   C William Caxton

   D William Shakespeare

8   Which of these statements is correct?

   A Refuges and shelters offer a safe place to stay for victims of domestic violence.

   B The Citizens Advice Bureau offers a safe place to stay for victims of domestic violence.

9   When were the first professional football clubs formed?

   A 17th century

   B 18th century

   C 19th century

   D 20th century

10 Which work of music did Benjamin Britten not write?

- **A** Peter Grimes
- **B** The Planets
- **C** Billy Budd
- **D** A Young Person's Guide to the Orchestra

11 Which of the following countries did not help to set up the EEC?

- **A** Ireland
- **B** Luxemburg
- **C** Belgium
- **D** Germany

12 Which of the following is a good way of helping your community?

- **A** Travelling
- **B** Complaining
- **C** Volunteering
- **D** Spending lots of time online

13 How are local authorities funded?

- **A** By funding from central government only
- **B** By taxation only
- **C** By central government funding and by taxation
- **D** Local authorities are unfunded

14 Which TWO of the following can offer information for people who believe they are suffering from discrimination?

- **A** The Equality Commission or Human Rights Commission
- **B** The local education authority
- **C** The Citizens Advice Bureau
- **D** The armed services

15   Which of these statements is correct?

A Everyone pays National Insurance Contributions.

B Most working people pay National Insurance Contributions.

16   What did William, Duke of Normandy, become?

A King of England

B King of France

C King of Scotland

D King of Wales

17   Sir Arthur Conan Doyle created which famous fictional detective?

A Sherlock Holmes

B Miss Marple

C Hercule Poirot

D Sam Spade

18   The UEFA Champions League pits British soccer teams against other teams from where?

A Europe

B USA

C South America

D Asia

19   Who chairs debates in the House of Commons?

A The leader of the opposition

B The Prime Minister

C The Speaker

D The Foreign Secretary

20 **Which of these is an accurate estimate of the number of casualties suffered by Britain in the First World War?**

- **A** 2 million
- **B** 10 million
- **C** 8 million
- **D** 500,000

21 **William Shakespeare wrote a number of sonnets. What are sonnets?**

- **A** Poems of 14 lines
- **B** Mystery plays
- **C** Rhyming poems
- **D** Stories for children

22 **Which of these figures indicating total UK population in various years is not correct?**

- **A** 1700 – 5 million
- **B** 1801 – 17 million
- **C** 1851 – 20 million
- **D** 1901 – 40 million

23 **Which of the following statements is correct?**

- **A** Police do not have the power to confiscate alcohol from people drinking in public.
- **B** Police have the power to confiscate alcohol from people drinking in public.

24 **Which of these national saints' days is incorrect?**

- **A** 1 March: St David's Day, Wales
- **B** 17 March: St Patrick's Day, Northern Ireland
- **C** 23 April: St George's Day, England
- **D** 1 November: St Matthew's Day, Scotland

ANSWERS: PRACTICE TEST 1

			Handbook reference	Study Guide reference
1	D	Jane Seymour	41	49
2	A	15	40–2	48–50
3	A	Chieftains became landlords if they had the favour of the English king	52–3	60–1
	C	Clansmen became tenants who had to pay for the land they used		
4	C	Northern Ireland	91	99
5	A	Snowdonia is a national park.	119	127
	C	The Lake District is England's largest national park.		
6	A	England, Wales, Scotland and Ireland	58	66
7	D	William Shakespeare	44	52
8	A	Refuges and shelters offer a safe place to stay for victims of domestic violence.	154	162
9	C	19th century	94–5	102–3
10	B	The Planets	97–9	105–7
11	A	Ireland	142	150
12	C	Volunteering	159	167
13	C	By central government funding and by taxation	133	141
14	A	The Equality Commission or Human Rights Commission	154	162
	C	The Citizens Advice Bureau		
15	B	Most working people pay National Insurance Contributions.	156	164
16	A	King of England	33	41
17	A	Sherlock Holmes	104	112
18	A	Europe	94–5	102–3
19	C	The Speaker	129–30	137–8
20	A	2 million	64–5	72–3
21	A	Poems of 14 lines	104–6	112–4
22	B	1801 – 17 million	82	90
23	B	Police have the power to confiscate alcohol from people drinking in public.	144–5	152–3
24	D	1 November: St Matthew's Day, Scotland	85–6	93–4

PRACTICE TEST 2

1 **Is the statement below TRUE or FALSE?**
*Military training for young people is provided
by The National Citizen Service.*

   A True

   B False

2 **Where can you find contact details for your elected representatives?**

   A From your doctor's surgery

   B From the UKBA

   C In the Phone Book or Yellow Pages

   D From the Department of Work and Pensions

3 **Which of these statements about
Isambard Kingdom Brunel is not true?**

   A He was born in Portsmouth and lived from 1806 to 1859.

   B He built tunnels, bridges, railway lines and ships.

   C He designed the Clifton Suspension Bridge that spans the Avon Gorge.

   D He became Prime Minister in 1840.

4 **An attempt by which group to put James II's son on the
throne instead of George I was quickly defeated?**

   A French Huguenots

   B Scottish Jacobites

   C Irish Catholics

   D English Puritans

5 **Is the statement below TRUE or FALSE?**
*The Bill of Rights confirmed the rights of Parliament
and the limits of the king's power.*

   A True

   B False

6 Charles I was unwilling to reach an agreement with Parliament. Following his defeat in the Civil war, what happened to him?

- **A** He was exiled
- **B** He was executed
- **C** He was exonerated
- **D** He was excommunicated

7 Is the statement below TRUE or FALSE?
Following the Emancipation Act of 1833, the Royal Navy stopped slave ships from other countries, killed the slave traders and gave the slaves the ships.

- **A** True
- **B** False

8 What were the lands in Ireland called that had been taken from Catholic landowners and subsequently colonised by Scottish and English Protestant settlers?

- **A** Settlements
- **B** Colonies
- **C** Plantations
- **D** Village

9 Which TWO of the following can provide the names of local solicitors and the area of law in which they specialise?

- **A** The local doctors' surgery
- **B** The Citizens Advice Bureau
- **C** The Law Society
- **D** The local authority

10 Is the statement below TRUE or FALSE?
Some people rent land away from home called an allotment, where they can grow fruit and vegetables.

- **A** True
- **B** False

11 Britain today is a diverse society, and post-war immigration means that how much of the population has a parent or grandparent born outside the UK?

   A 25%

   B 2%

   C 10%

   D 50%

12 During the reign of Henry VIII, which country of the union became formally united with England?

   A Ireland

   B Wales

   C Scotland

   D Northern Ireland

13 The judiciary is responsible for which TWO of the following?

   A Interpreting the law

   B Making the law

   C Arresting people

   D Making sure that trials are fair

14 Is the statement below TRUE or FALSE?
Norman French influenced the development of the English language as we know it today.

   A True

   B False

15 Which of the following statements is not correct?

   A Increasing German losses, coupled with American support, meant that soon the Allies were able to attack Normandy, in an operation often known as D-Day.

   B D-Day was an Allied operation that attacked German forces in France by advancing through Spain.

16   Which annual flower show in London exhibits garden designs from around the world?

A South Bank

B Covent Garden

C Chelsea

D Kensington

17   Where did the people of the Bronze Age bury their dead?

A Round burrows

B Round barrows

C Burial mounds

D Earth barrows

18   In a Crown Court, who decides what the penalty will be, in the case of a 'guilty' verdict?

A A solicitor

B The judge

C The jury

D A police officer

19   The free trade reforms of the Victorian period are said to have helped British industry. Why?

A They let workers move across the country more easily

B They helped establish better transport links

C They offered cheap government loans to factory owners

D They let foreign goods be imported more cheaply

20 **Sake Dean Mahomet returned to England at the turn of the century and in 1810 he opened which establishment in George Street, London?**

- **A** Hindoostane Coffee House
- **B** Hindoostane Curry House
- **C** Mahomet Coffee House
- **D** Mahomet Curry House

21 **Which of these is not a Christmas tradition in the UK?**

- **A** Giving gifts
- **B** Having a barbecue
- **C** Sending cards
- **D** Decorating houses and trees

22 **Catherine Parr married Henry VIII late in his life. Who died first?**

- **A** She died first and he never remarried
- **B** He died first and she was a widow for the rest of her life
- **C** She died in childbirth and Henry remarried
- **D** He died first and she went on to remarry

23 **Which of the following statements is correct?**

- **A** Elizabeth I came to the throne when, following a short reign, her half-sister Mary died.
- **B** Elizabeth I came to the throne when, following a long reign, her cousin Mary died.

24 **What is wrong with this statement?**
Julian Lloyd Webber, in collaboration with Tim Rice, wrote musicals such as Cats, The Phantom of the Opera and Evita.

- **A** 'Evita' is not a musical.
- **B** It was Tom Rice not Tim Rice who collaborated with him.
- **C** It was Andrew Lloyd Webber not Julian who was involved in writing these musicals.
- **D** Nothing is wrong with the statement.

ANSWERS: PRACTICE TEST 2

			Handbook reference	Study Guide reference
1	B	False	162–4	170–2
2	C	In the Phone Book or Yellow Pages	130	138
3	D	He became Prime Minister in 1840.	60	68
4	B	Scottish Jacobites	52–3	60–1
5	A	True	51	59
6	B	He was executed	46–8	54–6
7	B	False	55–6	63–4
8	C	Plantations	45	53
9	B	The Citizens Advice Bureau	152–3	160–1
	C	The Law Society		
10	A	True	106–7	114–5
11	C	10%	80	88
12	B	Wales	40–2	48–50
13	A	Interpreting the law	147–8	155–6
	D	Making sure that trials are fair		
14	A	True	33–4	41–2
15	B	D-Day was an Allied operation that attacked German forces in France by advancing through Spain.	66–9	74–7
16	C	Chelsea	102–3	110–1
17	B	Round barrows	30–1	38–9
18	B	The judge	148	156
19	D	They let foreign goods be imported more cheaply	59–60	67–8
20	A	Hindoostane Coffee House	55	63
21	B	Having a barbecue	87	95
22	D	He died first and she went on to remarry	41	49
23	A	Elizabeth I came to the throne when, following a short reign, her half-sister Mary died.	42–3	50–1
24	C	It was Andrew Lloyd Webber not Julian who was involved in writing these musicals.	99–100	107–8

PRACTICE TEST 3

1 On which type of surface are the Wimbledon Tennis Championships played?

- **A** Hard court
- **B** Grass
- **C** Clay
- **D** Indoor carpet

2 Which TWO of the following statements about the Norman conquest is correct?

- **A** The Normans were only interested in conquering English territory.
- **B** The Normans invaded Scotland unsuccessfully.
- **C** The Normans fought on the border of Scotland and England.
- **D** The Normans took over some land on the border between Scotland and England.

3 Which of these statements about Olympic gold medal winner Mary Peters is not true?

- **A** She won gold at the 1976 Olympics in the 200 metres.
- **B** She became team manager for the women's British Olympic team.
- **C** In 2000 she was made a Dame of the British Empire.
- **D** She moved to Northern Ireland as a child and continues to promote sport and tourism there.

4 Where does the UK Parliament sit?

- **A** Westminster
- **B** Downing Street
- **C** Stormont
- **D** The House of Lords

5   Which of the following statements is correct?

   A The 'Divine Right of Kings' was the view held by many English monarchs that they could seize lands belonging to the nobility as they wished.

   B The 'Divine Right of Kings' was the view held by many English monarchs that they were directly appointed by God to rule.

6   George Frederick Handel, the German-born composer who became a British citizen, wrote which of the following?

   A Balthazar's Feast

   B Peter Grimes

   C The Planets

   D Music for the Royal Fireworks

7   The Wars of the Roses was fought by the supporters of which TWO families in order to decide who should be King of England?

   A The House of Lancaster

   B The House of Windsor

   C The House of York

   D The House of Tudor

8   Churchill lost the post-war election but returned as Prime Minister in which year?

   A 1951

   B 1947

   C 1946

   D 1955

9   Are police obliged to obey the law?

   A Yes, except when investigating a difficult case

   B Yes, always

10 **King James II of England, Wales and Ireland was also which King James of Scotland?**

  A I

  B II

  C V

  D VII

11 **How often is a General Election held?**

  A Every year

  B At least every two years

  C At least every four years

  D At least every five years

12 **Who controlled England immediately after Charles I was executed?**

  A No one

  B Oliver Cromwell

  C The army

  D The nobility

13 **What were the consequences of the Black Death in Britain?**

  A The plague destroyed cereal crops, leading to a famine

  B There were labour shortages and people began to demand higher wages

  C All the people who spoke Norman French were killed, so Anglo-Saxon was the only language spoken

  D The power to change the law was taken away from the monarch

14 **What is the capital city of Northern Ireland?**

  A Belfast

  B Dublin

  C The Pale

  D Edinburgh

15 What is New Year's Eve called in Scotland?

- **A** Hopmanay
- **B** Hogmanay
- **C** Hagmanay
- **D** Hugmanay

16 Who or what were the 'clans'?

- **A** English Lords
- **B** Welsh landowners
- **C** Prominent families in Scotland and Ireland
- **D** Prominent families in England and Wales

17 Who was James II's eldest daughter, Mary, married to?

- **A** Her cousin, William of Orange
- **B** The Duke of York
- **C** The French Dauphin
- **D** She never married

18 Britain was brought into conflict with which country during the 19th century, because they were expanding and trading in similar areas?

- **A** Germany
- **B** The Netherlands
- **C** Spain
- **D** France

19 How many steps were in the 1935 film directed by Alfred Hitchcock?

- **A** 21
- **B** 39
- **C** 100
- **D** 1,001

20 **Is the statement below TRUE or FALSE?**
Members of the House of Lords are elected by a constituency.

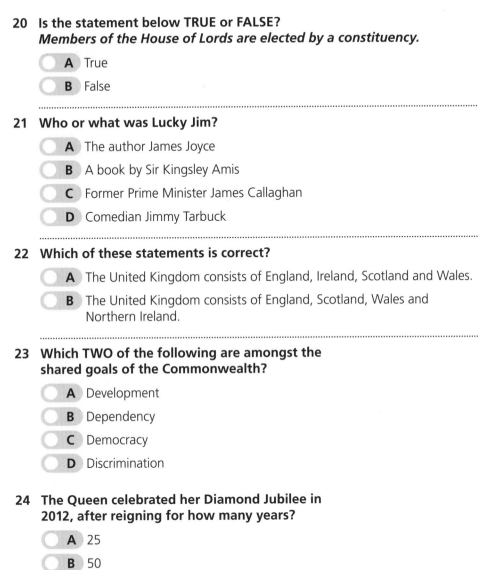

A True

B False

21 **Who or what was Lucky Jim?**

A The author James Joyce

B A book by Sir Kingsley Amis

C Former Prime Minister James Callaghan

D Comedian Jimmy Tarbuck

22 **Which of these statements is correct?**

A The United Kingdom consists of England, Ireland, Scotland and Wales.

B The United Kingdom consists of England, Scotland, Wales and Northern Ireland.

23 **Which TWO of the following are amongst the shared goals of the Commonwealth?**

A Development

B Dependency

C Democracy

D Discrimination

24 **The Queen celebrated her Diamond Jubilee in 2012, after reigning for how many years?**

A 25

B 50

C 60

D 70

ANSWERS: PRACTICE TEST 3

			Handbook reference	Study Guide reference
1	B	Grass	96	104
2	C	The Normans fought on the border of Scotland and England.	33–4	41–2
	D	The Normans took over some land on the border between Scotland and England.		
3	A	She won gold at the 1976 Olympics in the 200 metres.	75	83
4	A	Westminster	26	34
5	B	The 'Divine Right of Kings' was the view held by many English monarchs that they were directly appointed by God to rule.	45–6	53–4
6	D	Music for the Royal Fireworks	97–9	105–7
7	A	The House of Lancaster	39	47
	C	The House of York		
8	A	1951	68	76
9	B	Yes, always	145–6	153–4
10	D	VII	49	57
11	D	At least every five years	130	138
12	C	The army	46–8	54–6
13	B	There were labour shortages and people began to demand higher wages	35–6	43–4
14	A	Belfast	81	89
15	B	Hogmanay	53	61
16	C	Prominent families in Scotland and Ireland	35–6	43–4
17	A	Her cousin, William of Orange	49–50	57–8
18	D	France	53–5	61–3
19	B	39	109	117
20	B	False	129	137
21	B	A book by Sir Kingsley Amis	104	112
22	B	The United Kingdom consists of England, Scotland, Wales and Northern Ireland.	26	34
23	A	Development	141	149
	C	Democracy		
24	C	60	125–7	133–5

PRACTICE TEST 4

1 Is the statement below TRUE or FALSE?
Under the system of feudalism, the kings gave land to lords, and the landowners had to send men to serve in the army in return.

A True

B False

2 Is a verdict of 'not proven' possible?

A Yes, but only in a Magistrates' Court

B Yes, but only in Scotland

3 Is the statement below TRUE or FALSE?
Jane Austen and Charles Dickens were both famous sculptors.

A True

B False

4 What is the full title of the European Convention on Human Rights?

A The European Convention on Human and Animal Rights

B The European Convention on Human and State Rights

C The European Convention on Human Rights and Fundamental Freedoms

D The European Convention on Human Rights and Government Freedoms

5 Is the statement below TRUE or FALSE?
Adult citizens of other EU states may vote in General Elections.

A True

B False

6 **After the Act of Union, Scotland was no longer an independent country. In what ways was it still separate from the rest of Great Britain?**

- **A** It kept its own legal system
- **B** It kept its own educational system
- **C** It kept its own Presbyterian church
- **D** All of the above

7 **Who or what are 'Vets'?**

- **A** A British team playing American football
- **B** Very experienced teachers
- **C** Veterinary surgeons
- **D** Support staff in local medical centres

8 **Is the statement below TRUE or FALSE?**
Richard Arkwright developed horse-driven spinning mills that used only one machine, increasing efficiency and production.

- **A** True
- **B** False

9 **Which of these books did Graham Greene not write?**

- **A** The Honorary Consul
- **B** Brighton Rock
- **C** Moby Dick
- **D** The Heart of the Matter

10 **Who were Elizabeth I's parents?**

- **A** Henry VII and Elizabeth of York
- **B** Henry VIII and Catherine of Aragon
- **C** Henry VIII and Jane Seymour
- **D** Henry VIII and Anne Boleyn

11 In 1948 Aneurin (Nye) Bevan led the establishment of the National Health Service (NHS). What was his role at the time?

- **A** Minister for Health
- **B** Deputy Prime Minister
- **C** Home Secretary
- **D** Minister for Social Security

12 What was the main source of employment in the UK before the Industrial Revolution?

- **A** Agriculture
- **B** The wool trade
- **C** Financial services
- **D** Canal building

13 Which of the following statements is correct?

- **A** The jet engine and radar were developed in Britain in the 1950s.
- **B** The jet engine and radar were developed in Britain in the 1930s.

14 Is the statement below TRUE or FALSE?
By around AD 600, Anglo-Saxon kingdoms were established in Britain.

- **A** True
- **B** False

15 In 1649, England was declared a republic. What was it called?

- **A** The Commonwealth
- **B** The People's Republic
- **C** Cromwell's Republic
- **D** Great Britain

16 Which TWO of the following were members of the Royal Society?

A Sir Christopher Wren

B Samuel Pepys

C Sir Edmond Halley

D Sir Isaac Newton

17 Is it acceptable in the UK to treat people worse because of their sexual orientation?

A Yes, if their sexual orientation is forbidden by religion

B No, it is never acceptable to treat people worse for their sexual orientation

18 Queen Elizabeth II is the head of state for which TWO of the following?

A The United Kingdom

B The European Union

C Iceland

D Many Commonwealth countries

19 Is the statement below TRUE or FALSE?
Sir Robert Walpole was Prime Minister from 1700–1730.

A True

B False

20 A snack made from flour, dried fruits and spices and served either hot or cold is which of the following?

A A Scottish bun

B An English muffin

C An Irish pie

D A Welsh cake

21 **What is the name of the famous horse race held near Liverpool?**

A Grand Chase

B Grand Derby

C Steeplechase

D Grand National

22 **NATO is a group of North American and European countries that have agreed to do which TWO of the following?**

A Promote peace between member countries

B Promote traditional culture

C Protect each other when under attack

D Allow the free movement of people across borders

23 **Is the statement below TRUE or FALSE?**
Commercial expansion and prosperity of the 19th century were sustained in part by the booming slave trade.

A True

B False

24 **Is the statement below TRUE or FALSE?**
You have to be 16 or over to buy a drink in a public house (pub) or nightclub.

A True

B False

ANSWERS: PRACTICE TEST 4

			Handbook reference	Study Guide reference
1	A	True	35–6	43–4
2	B	Yes, but only in Scotland	148–9	156–7
3	B	False	104	112
4	C	The European Convention on Human Rights and Fundamental Freedoms	143	151
5	B	False	138	146
6	B	It kept its own educational system	52	60
7	C	Veterinary surgeons	112	120
8	A	True	54	62
9	C	Moby Dick	104	112
10	D	Henry VIII and Anne Boleyn	40–2	48–50
11	A	Minister for Health	70–1	78–9
12	A	Agriculture	53–5	61–3
13	B	The jet engine and radar were developed in Britain in the 1930s.	74–5	82–3
14	A	True	31–3	39–41
15	A	The Commonwealth	46–8	54–6
16	C	Sir Edmond Halley	48	56
	D	Sir Isaac Newton		
17	B	No, it is never acceptable to treat people worse for their sexual orientation	158	166
18	A	The United Kingdom	125–7	133–5
	D	Many Commonwealth countries		
19	B	False	52	60
20	D	A Welsh cake	108	116
21	D	Grand National	95	103
22	A	Promote peace between member countries	143	151
	C	Protect each other when under attack		
23	A	True	55–6	63–4
24	B	False	111	119

PRACTICE TEST 5

1   Is the statement below TRUE or FALSE?
*The police do not need to protect and help
people who are not UK citizens.*

A   True

B   False

2   Is the statement below TRUE or FALSE?
The Channel Islands and the Isle of Man are part of the UK.

A   True

B   False

3   Is the statement below TRUE or FALSE?
*The Puritans agreed with the religious reforms of the
Church of England introduced by Charles I.*

A   True

B   False

**4   Which Catherine was executed after being
accused of taking lovers by Henry VIII?**

A   Parr

B   Boleyn

C   Of Aragon

D   Howard

**5   Someone wishing to stand as a candidate for election
as an MP would need to be how old?**

A   16

B   18

C   21

D   There is no minimum age limit

6 Sir Anthony Van Dyck was famous as which of the following?

- **A** Actor
- **B** Painter
- **C** Sculptor
- **D** Composer

7 Which of the following takes place on 14 February every year?

- **A** St Christopher's Day
- **B** St George's Day
- **C** St Valentine's Day
- **D** All Saints Day

8 Which of the following statements is correct?

- **A** Chequers is the Prime Minister's country house.
- **B** Chequers is the Prime Minister's house in London.

9 Where did Florence Nightingale establish the Nightingale School for Nurses in 1860?

- **A** St Thomas' Hospital, London
- **B** Addenbrooke's Hospital, Cambridge
- **C** St James's University Hospital, Leeds
- **D** Prince Philip Hospital, Llanelli

10 What are small Scottish farms also known as?

- **A** Crofts
- **B** Bothies
- **C** Hamlets
- **D** Homesteads

11 Ian McEwan, Hilary Mantel and Julian Barnes have all won the Man Booker Prize for which type of literature?

- **A** Factual
- **B** Fiction
- **C** Biography
- **D** Autobiography

12 For much of the Stone Age, Britain was connected to the continent by what?

- **A** A bridge
- **B** A land bridge
- **C** A glacier
- **D** A tunnel

13 Who usually plays the part of a pantomime dame?

- **A** A woman
- **B** A man
- **C** A celebrity
- **D** A child

14 In what way was Elizabeth I skilled at managing Parliament?

- **A** She balanced her views with the views of the increasingly Protestant House of Commons and House of Lords
- **B** She reduced the power of Parliament so her wishes had more significance
- **C** She banned Catholics from the House of Commons
- **D** She executed those who opposed her

15 **The National Assembly makes laws for Wales in 20 areas. It does not make laws in which of the following areas?**

- **A** Housing
- **B** Economic policy
- **C** Education and training
- **D** Health and social services

16 **Diwali is a religious celebration for which TWO religious groups?**

- **A** Jews
- **B** Muslims
- **C** Sikhs
- **D** Hindus

17 **Is the statement below TRUE or FALSE?**
In the Middle Ages, England's system of 'common law' was established by referring to previous decisions and tradition.

- **A** True
- **B** False

18 **Who became Prime Minister in May 2010?**

- **A** David Cameron
- **B** Nick Clegg
- **C** Ed Miliband
- **D** Nigel Farage

19 **The Festival of Lights is a non-Christian festival known as which of the following?**

- **A** Vaisakhi
- **B** Hannukah
- **C** Diwali
- **D** Eid ul Adha

20 Where are details about small claims procedures available?

- **A** Your local police station
- **B** Your local supermarket
- **C** County Court or Sheriff Court
- **D** The NHS

21 In which year did Oliver Cromwell die?

- **A** 1658
- **B** 1758
- **C** 1608
- **D** 1708

22 What is Ridley Scott famous for?

- **A** Directing films
- **B** Theatre production
- **C** Conducting orchestras
- **D** Singing as an operatic tenor

23 Is the statement below TRUE or FALSE?
The UK is a parliamentary democracy.

- **A** True
- **B** False

24 Which of the following statements is correct?

- **A** Murder, assault and theft are crimes.
- **B** Murder, assault and theft are examples of civil disputes.

ANSWERS: PRACTICE TEST 5

			Handbook reference	Study Guide reference
1	B	False	145–6	153–4
2	B	False	26	34
3	B	False	46	54
4	D	Howard	41	49
5	B	18	132	140
6	B	Painter	100–1	108–9
7	C	St Valentine's Day	90	98
8	A	Chequers is the Prime Minister's country house.	131	139
9	A	St Thomas' Hospital, London	61	69
10	A	Crofts	52–3	60–1
11	B	Fiction	103	111
12	B	A land bridge	30–1	38–9
13	B	A man	99–100	107–8
14	A	She balanced her views with the views of the increasingly Protestant House of Commons and House of Lords	45–6	53–4
15	B	Economic policy	133–7	141–5
16	C	Sikhs	88	96
	D	Hindus		
17	A	True	36–7	44–5
18	A	David Cameron	78	86
19	C	Diwali	88	96
20	C	County Court or Sheriff Court	151	159
21	A	1658	46–8	54–6
22	A	Directing films	108–9	116–7
23	A	True	128	136
24	A	Murder, assault and theft are crimes.	144–5	152–3

PRACTICE TEST 6

1 **Which period of British history saw the emergence of a national culture and identity?**

- **A** The Bronze Age
- **B** The Middle Ages
- **C** The Victorian period
- **D** The Tudor period

2 **What is the capital city of the UK?**

- **A** Birmingham
- **B** Liverpool
- **C** London
- **D** Sheffield

3 **The first four-minute mile was achieved by Sir Roger Bannister in which decade of the 20th century?**

- **A** The forties
- **B** The fifties
- **C** The sixties
- **D** The seventies

4 **Many British people were encouraged to settle overseas during and immediately after Victoria's reign. What is a reasonable estimate for the numbers that left the UK between 1853 and 1913?**

- **A** 100,000
- **B** 13 million
- **C** 500 million
- **D** 2 million

5 **Which of the following statements is correct?**

A The declaration of rights read at the coronation of William and Mary meant the monarch could no longer raise taxes or administer justice.

B The declaration of rights read at the coronation of William and Mary meant the monarch had absolute power to rule without the interference of Parliament.

6 **When did Dame Ellen MacArthur become the fastest person to sail single-handed around the world?**

A 1974

B 1984

C 1994

D 2004

7 **When did the Boer War take place?**

A 1899 to 1902

B 1910 to 1913

C 1885 to 1888

D 1890 to 1893

8 **Richard Arkwright used steam engines to do what?**

A Pull carriages

B Power machinery

C Create electricity

D All of the above

9 **Henry VIII took which title in relation to Ireland?**

A Head

B King

C Lieutenant

D Commander

10 Which of the following statements is correct?

- **A** The predominantly Protestant Scottish Parliament welcomed the authority of the Pope in Scotland and Roman Catholic religious services became commonplace.

- **B** The predominantly Protestant Scottish Parliament abolished the authority of the Pope in Scotland and Roman Catholic religious services became illegal.

11 Which of the following would be dealt with by a Magistrates' Court rather than a Crown Court?

- **A** All of the most serious criminal cases

- **B** The majority of the most serious criminal cases

- **C** The majority of minor criminal offences

- **D** A Magistrates' Court does not deal with any criminal cases

12 Eid al-Fitr celebrates the end of Ramadan. For how long before do Muslims fast?

- **A** Five days

- **B** Two weeks

- **C** One month

- **D** Twenty-one days

13 The National Eisteddfod is a major cultural festival that takes place in which country?

- **A** England

- **B** Scotland

- **C** Wales

- **D** Northern Ireland

14 Is the statement below TRUE or FALSE?
The threat of Viking attack caused the peoples in the north to unite, and the term Scotland was used to describe that country.

- **A** True

- **B** False

15 The British equivalent of the Oscars is hosted by BAFTA. What do these initials stand for?

   A British Association of Film and Technical Appliances

   B British Academy of Film and Theatre Awards

   C British Academy of Film and Television Arts

   D British Awards for Film and Television Actors

16 What information must always be entered on an electoral registration form?

   A Only the names of adult men resident at the address

   B The names of everyone at the address

   C The names of all eligible voters who live at the address

   D Only the names of adult women resident at the address

17 Who is the ceremonial head of the Commonwealth?

   A The Prime Minister

   B The President of the USA

   C The Queen

   D The Prince of Wales

18 The French Wars ended in 1815 when Napoleon was defeated by the Duke of Wellington at which battle?

   A Battle of Waterloo

   B Battle of Trafalgar

   C Battle of Ostend

   D Battle of Naseby

19 Which Anglo-Saxon poem tells of its hero's battles against monsters?

   A Beowulf

   B The Fight at Finnsburh

   C Waldere

   D Deor

20 Which of the following statements about Britain in the 1930s is true?

A The first cars were sold in the UK between 1930 and 1939.

B Writers such as Thomas Hardy became prominent.

C John Maynard Keynes published influential theories of economics.

D Adolf Hitler came to power in Austria in 1933.

21 To apply to become a permanent resident or citizen of the UK, you will need to be able to do which TWO of the following?

A Speak and read English

B Speak and read Welsh

C Have a good understanding of life in the UK

D Speak more than one language

22 Which of the following is a famous British film?

A Passport to Paddington

B Passport to Portsmouth

C Passport to Panama

D Passport to Pimlico

23 The right for every adult male and female to vote is usually known as what?

A Universal balloting

B Universal democracy

C Universal voting rights

D Universal suffrage

24 Every MP represents which of the following?

A A constituency

B A county

C A city

D None of the above

ANSWERS: PRACTICE TEST 6

			Handbook reference	Study Guide reference
1	B	The Middle Ages	37–9	45–7
2	C	London	81	89
3	B	The fifties	92–3	100–1
4	B	13 million	59	67
5	A	The declaration of rights read at the coronation of William and Mary meant the monarch could no longer raise taxes or administer justice.	51	59
6	D	2004	92–3	100–1
7	A	1899 to 1902	63	71
8	B	Power machinery	54	62
9	B	King	45	53
10	B	The predominantly Protestant Scottish Parliament abolished the authority of the Pope in Scotland and Roman Catholic religious services became illegal.	43	51
11	C	The majority of minor criminal offences	148–9	156–7
12	C	One month	89	97
13	C	Wales	97–9	105–7
14	A	True	33	41
15	C	British Academy of Film and Television Arts	108–9	116–7
16	C	The names of all eligible voters who live at the address	138–9	146–7
17	C	The Queen	141	149
18	A	Battle of Waterloo	56–7	64–5
19	A	Beowulf	104–5	112–3
20	C	John Maynard Keynes published influential theories of economics.	66	74
21	A	Speak and read English	21–2	29–30
	C	Have a good understanding of life in the UK		
22	D	Passport to Pimlico	108–9	116–7
23	D	Universal suffrage	61–2	69–70
24	A	A constituency	128	136

PRACTICE TEST 7

1   Who were the Huguenots?

- **A** Roman Catholics
- **B** French Catholics
- **C** Dutch Protestants
- **D** French Protestants

2   Is this statement TRUE or FALSE?
There are now more women in high-level positions than ever before, including senior managers in traditionally male-dominated occupations.

- **A** True
- **B** False

3   Who wrote the poem The Tyger?

- **A** William Wordsworth
- **B** William Blake
- **C** William Shakespeare
- **D** William Wallace

4   Which of the following statements is correct?

- **A** Robert Burns wrote only in Scots language.
- **B** Robert Burns wrote in Scots, English and a combination of both.

5   Since which year has the Prime Minister had the power to nominate life peers to the House of Lords?

- **A** 1925
- **B** 1958
- **C** 1999
- **D** 2012

6 Which of these statements is correct?

    A All the national saints' days are celebrated but only in Scotland and Northern Ireland are they official holidays.

    B All the national saints' days are celebrated but only in England and Wales are they official holidays.

7 Is it possible for parents or other community groups to open a free school?

    A Yes, in any part of the UK

    B Yes, but only in England

8 Which of the following will help you get along with your neighbours?

    A Only putting rubbish and recycling out on collection days

    B Having an untidy garden

    C Making lots of noise, especially late at night

    D Only introducing yourself to them after a year

9 Is the statement below TRUE or FALSE?
Cricket is the UK's most popular sport.

    A True

    B False

10 Since which year has the UK had a fully democratic voting system?

    A 1889

    B 1918

    C 1928

    D 1969

11   The Welsh Assembly and the Scottish Parliament were formed in which year?

    A 1997

    B 1999

    C 2003

    D 2008

12   Is the statement below TRUE or FALSE?
France was the first country to industrialise on a large scale.

    A True

    B False

13   Which of these reasons best explains why town planning laws were tightened in the early 20th century?

    A To protect the countryside

    B To stop skyscrapers being built

    C To allow for the building of new churches

    D To prevent the further development of slums

14   Is the statement below TRUE or FALSE?
Thanks to its position as the world's leading industrial nation during the 1800s, Britain was responsible for producing half of the world's coal, iron and cotton cloth.

    A True

    B False

15   How often is Prime Minister's Questions held?

    A Every day

    B Every day while Parliament is in session

    C Every week

    D Every week while Parliament is in session

16   Which of the following statements is correct?

A People in the UK are living longer than ever before, with a record number living until over 85, thanks to improved health care and living standards. This has an impact on the cost of pensions and health care.

B The average lifespan for UK residents is steadily decreasing, which saves the government money on pensions and health care.

17   The Royal Society was formed to promote what?

A Astronomy

B Natural knowledge

C Art

D Medicine

18   Who is the head of state?

A The President

B The Prime Minister

C Prince Philip

D The Queen

19   Which TWO events happened to the church in England following the restoration of Charles II?

A The Church of England was restored as the official Church

B The Puritans and Roman Catholics were kept out of power

C The Puritans grew in strength and number

D The Church of England was suppressed

20 **If the following headline appeared in a newspaper, which date would you think it was?**
'Martians land at Heathrow Airport in a large spaceship and have captured the British Prime Minister.'

A 1 January

B 1 March

C 1 April

D 1 May

21 **Is the statement below TRUE or FALSE?**
You must always tell a canvasser how you intend to vote.

A True

B False

22 **Margaret Thatcher was famous for her close working relationship with which American President?**

A Woodrow Wilson

B Gerald Ford

C Bill Clinton

D Ronald Reagan

23 **Which of the following statements is correct?**

A Thomas Chippendale was an 18th-century designer of furniture.

B Sir Terence Conran was an 18th-century designer of furniture.

24 **John Petts was a Welshman famous in which of these TWO areas of art?**

A Stained glass

B Water colours

C Engraving

D Paintings of horses

ANSWERS: PRACTICE TEST 7

			Handbook reference	Study Guide reference
1	D	French Protestants	52	60
2	A	True	83–4	91–2
3	B	William Blake	104–6	112–4
4	B	Robert Burns wrote in Scots, English and a combination of both.	53	61
5	B	1958	129	137
6	A	All the national saints' days are celebrated but only in Scotland and Northern Ireland are they official holidays.	85–6	93–4
7	B	Yes, but only in England	159–61	167–9
8	A	Only putting rubbish and recycling out on collection days	159	167
9	B	False	94	102
10	C	1928	138	146
11	B	1999	133–7	141–5
12	B	False	53–5	61–3
13	D	To prevent the further development of slums	64–5	72–3
14	A	True	59–60	67–8
15	D	Every week while Parliament is in session	132	140
16	A	People in the UK are living longer than ever before, with a record number living until over 85, thanks to improved health care and living standards. This has an impact on the cost of pensions and health care.	83	91
17	B	Natural knowledge	48	56
18	D	The Queen	125–7	133–5
19	A	The Church of England was restored as the official Church	48	56
	B	The Puritans and Roman Catholics were kept out of power		
20	C	1 April	90	98
21	B	False	161	169
22	D	Ronald Reagan	76	84
23	A	Thomas Chippendale was an 18th-century designer of furniture.	103	111
24	A	Stained glass	101	109
	C	Engraving		

PRACTICE TEST 8

1 **The Chancellor of the Exchequer is responsible for which area of government policy?**

- **A** Immigration
- **B** Education
- **C** Economy
- **D** Health

2 **The Scottish Parliament can make laws in which of the following areas?**

- **A** Health
- **B** Taxation
- **C** Civil and criminal law
- **D** All of the above

3 **The UK is a permanent member of the UN Security Council. How many permanent members does the Security Council have?**

- **A** 5
- **B** 15
- **C** 27
- **D** 190

4 **In the year 1600 the population of the UK stood at what?**

- **A** Just over 500,000
- **B** Just over 4 million
- **C** Just over 1 million
- **D** Just over 2 million

5 **On his escape from the Battle of Worcester, Charles II famously hid inside what?**

    A A forest

    B An oak tree

    C A cellar

    D None of the above

6 **The heptathlon comprises how many different track and field events?**

    A 5

    B 6

    C 7

    D 8

7 **Which statement describes 'party politics' during the reign of William and Mary?**

    A There were two main groups, the Liberals and the Conservatives.

    B There were two main groups, the Tories and the Whigs.

8 **Which of the following is not the job of the police?**

    A To prosecute someone for debt

    B To keep the peace

    C To prevent and detect crime

    D To protect life and property

9 **Is the statement below TRUE or FALSE?**
All Acts of Parliament are made in the name of the Prime Minister.

    A True

    B False

10 **After William III, Parliament was still some way from being a democracy. Why?**

   A Only bishops were able to vote

   B Only men who owned property of a certain value could vote

   C Only women were allowed to vote

   D Parliament took control of who could be monarch

11 **Who was king of England at the time of the Norman invasion in 1066?**

   A Herbert

   B Hubert

   C Harold

   D Henry

12 **Which of the following is a line from one of Churchill's famous speeches?**

   A I have a dream

   B The lady's not for turning

   C The only thing we have to fear is fear itself

   D I have nothing to offer but blood, toil, tears and sweat

13 **Which TWO of the following are freedoms offered to citizens and permanent residents of the UK?**

   A Freedom of speech

   B Half day off work on Friday

   C A right to take part in the election of a government

   D Free heating for all

14 **In which city is the Scottish Parliament based?**

   A Sheffield

   B Edinburgh

   C Glasgow

   D Cardiff

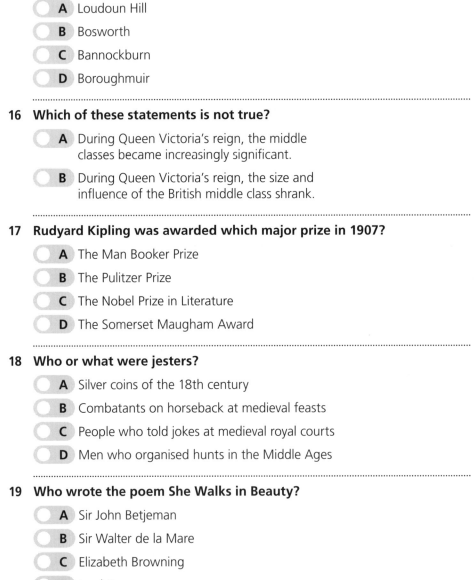

15 Scottish poet John Barbour's poem The Bruce was written about which battle?

- **A** Loudoun Hill
- **B** Bosworth
- **C** Bannockburn
- **D** Boroughmuir

16 Which of these statements is not true?

- **A** During Queen Victoria's reign, the middle classes became increasingly significant.
- **B** During Queen Victoria's reign, the size and influence of the British middle class shrank.

17 Rudyard Kipling was awarded which major prize in 1907?

- **A** The Man Booker Prize
- **B** The Pulitzer Prize
- **C** The Nobel Prize in Literature
- **D** The Somerset Maugham Award

18 Who or what were jesters?

- **A** Silver coins of the 18th century
- **B** Combatants on horseback at medieval feasts
- **C** People who told jokes at medieval royal courts
- **D** Men who organised hunts in the Middle Ages

19 Who wrote the poem She Walks in Beauty?

- **A** Sir John Betjeman
- **B** Sir Walter de la Mare
- **C** Elizabeth Browning
- **D** Lord Byron

20 **Is the statement below TRUE or FALSE?**
The Education Act of 1944 is often called The Butler Act and
introduced free secondary education in England and Wales.

- **A** True
- **B** False

21 **What are members of the Northern Ireland Parliament known as?**

- **A** MPs
- **B** MNIPs
- **C** MLAs
- **D** MEPs

22 **Which of these films was directed by David Lean?**

- **A** Women in Love
- **B** Four Weddings and a Funeral
- **C** The Killing Fields
- **D** Brief Encounter

23 **What is the common name for the Yeoman**
Warders at the Tower of London?

- **A** Pikestaff
- **B** Queen's Men
- **C** Crown Guards
- **D** Beefeaters

24 **Is the statement below TRUE or FALSE?**
A mayor is always elected.

- **A** True
- **B** False

ANSWERS: PRACTICE TEST 8

			Handbook reference	Study Guide reference
1	C	Economy	131–2	139–40
2	A	Health	133–7	141–5
3	A	5	143	151
4	B	Just over 4 million	82	90
5	B	An oak tree	46–8	54–6
6	C	7	92–3	100–1
7	B	There were two main groups, the Tories and the Whigs.	51	59
8	A	To prosecute someone for debt	145–6	153–4
9	B	False	125–7	133–5
10	B	Only men who owned property of a certain value could vote	51	59
11	C	Harold	33	41
12	D	I have nothing to offer but blood, toil, tears and sweat	68	76
13	A	Freedom of speech	20–1	28–9
	C	A right to take part in the election of a government		
14	B	Edinburgh	133–7	141–5
15	C	Bannockburn	37–9	45–7
16	B	During Queen Victoria's reign, the size and influence of the British middle class shrank.	59	67
17	C	The Nobel Prize in Literature	63	71
18	C	People who told jokes at medieval royal courts	109–10	117–8
19	D	Lord Byron	104–5	112–3
20	A	True	72	80
21	C	MLAs	140–1	148–9
22	D	Brief Encounter	109	117
23	D	Beefeaters	120	128
24	B	False	133	141

PRACTICE TEST 9

1   Which of the following statements is correct?

   A   The United Nations was set up between the
         First and Second World Wars.

   B   The United Nations was set up after the Second World War.

2   What was inscribed on some Iron Age coins?

   A   Dates

   B   Values

   C   Names of Iron Age kings

   D   Names of Iron Age settlements

**3   During the 16th century, which TWO factors predominantly
led to a bloody rebellion by the Irish chieftains?**

   A   Extreme poverty and famine

   B   The imposing of English laws on land inheritance

   C   High taxes on landowners

   D   The imposing of Protestantism

4   Henry VIII had six wives. What was the name of his first wife?

   A   Anne of Cleves

   B   Catherine Howard

   C   Catherine of Aragon

   D   Anne Boleyn

**5   The Northern Ireland Assembly was elected in 1999,
suspended in 2002 and reinstated in which year?**

   A   2003

   B   2005

   C   2007

   D   2010

6 Which of these TWO countries did poet and author Rudyard Kipling spend time living in?

- **A** India
- **B** Japan
- **C** Fiji
- **D** USA

7 Is the statement below TRUE or FALSE?
The Canterbury Tales was one of the first books to be printed by William Caxton.

- **A** True
- **B** False

8 Acts of Parliament in 1870 and 1882 awarded which right to women?

- **A** The right to bear arms
- **B** The right to work
- **C** The right to attend university
- **D** The right to keep their own earnings and property after marriage

9 During the early 1970s, Britain admitted 28,000 people of Indian origin who had been forced to leave where?

- **A** The West Indies
- **B** South Africa
- **C** China
- **D** Uganda

10 To go into a betting shop or casino, you have to be what age?

- **A** 15
- **B** 16
- **C** 17
- **D** 18

11   Which of these is not a Gilbert and Sullivan comic opera?

   A The Pirates of Penzance

   B The Mikado

   C The King and I

   D HMS Pinafore

12   William of Normandy invaded England in 1066. Where is Normandy?

   A Southern Scotland

   B Denmark

   C Northern France

   D Norway

13   Causing trouble whilst drinking in public can result in which TWO of the following from the police?

   A An award

   B Arrest

   C A fine

   D Praise

14   The English Parliament during the reign of Charles I contained many Puritans. What did the Puritans believe in?

   A Simple and strict religious doctrine and worship

   B Roman Catholic religious doctrine and worship

   C The power of the nobility to control Parliament

   D None of the above

15   Which of the statements below is correct?

   A Polling places or stations are open between 7am and 10pm.

   B Polling places or stations are open between 6am and 8pm.

16 Which of the following statements is correct?

A Big Ben is the clock at the Houses of Parliament.

B Big Ben is the tower in which the clock at the Houses of Parliament is installed.

C Big Ben refers to the name of the man who designed the clock at the Houses of Parliament.

D Big Ben refers to the great bell of the clock at the Houses of Parliament.

17 Around which structure in London is the Remembrance Day service usually held?

A The statue of Eros in Piccadilly Circus

B Nelson's Column in Trafalgar Square

C The London Eye

D The Cenotaph in Whitehall

18 Which of the following statements is correct?

A Dogs in public places must wear a muzzle.

B Dogs in public places must wear a collar showing the owner's name and address.

C Cats in public places must wear a collar.

D All dog owners must have a licence to keep their pets.

19 Is the statement below TRUE or FALSE?
The Welsh Assembly originally had substantial powers to legislate, whilst the Scottish Parliament was given fewer legislative powers but considerable control over public services.

A True

B False

20 **In which year was Wales annexed to the Crown of England by King Edward I of England?**

- **A** 1256
- **B** 1273
- **C** 1284
- **D** 1215

21 **Which of the following statements is correct?**

- **A** Colonists in North America were well educated and interested in ideas of liberty.
- **B** Colonists in North America were poorly educated and uninterested in politics.

22 **Where did Mary Stuart spend most of her childhood?**

- **A** France
- **B** Germany
- **C** Spain
- **D** England

23 **The UK has what kind of monarchy?**

- **A** Democratically elected
- **B** Constitutional
- **C** Provisional
- **D** Absolute

24 **Is the statement below TRUE or FALSE?**
The candidate who wins the most votes is elected MP for the constituency.

- **A** True
- **B** False

ANSWERS: PRACTICE TEST 9

			Handbook reference	Study Guide reference
1	B	The United Nations was set up after the Second World War.	143	151
2	C	Names of Iron Age kings	30–31	38–39
3	B	The imposing of English laws on land inheritance	40–2	48–50
	D	The imposing of Protestantism		
4	C	Catherine of Aragon	41	49
5	C	2007	77	85
6	A	India	63	71
	D	USA		
7	A	True	37–9	45–7
8	D	The right to keep their own earnings and property after marriage	61–2	69–70
9	D	Uganda	73	81
10	D	18	111	119
11	C	The King and I	99–100	106–7
12	C	Northern France	33	41
13	B	Arrest	144–5	152–3
	C	A fine		
14	A	Simple and strict religious doctrine and worship	46	54
15	A	Polling places or stations are open between 7am and 10pm.	139	147
16	D	Big Ben refers to the great bell of the clock at the Houses of Parliament.	113	121
17	D	The Cenotaph in Whitehall	90	98
18	B	Dogs in public places must wear a collar showing the owner's name and address.	112	120
19	B	False	77	85
20	C	1284	35	43
21	A	Colonists in North America were well educated and interested in ideas of liberty.	56	64
22	A	France	43	51
23	B	Constitutional	125–7	133–5
24	A	True	130	138

PRACTICE TEST 10

1 The first farmers probably came to Britain from where?

- **A** Norway
- **B** South-east Europe
- **C** North America
- **D** North-west Europe

2 In which of these years did Britain not host the Olympic Games?

- **A** 1908
- **B** 1928
- **C** 1948
- **D** 2012

3 How many people make up a Scottish jury?

- **A** 10
- **B** 12
- **C** 15
- **D** 20

4 What is a Yorkshire Pudding?

- **A** A caramel-flavoured dessert
- **B** Meat and potato in a pastry
- **C** Batter cooked in the oven
- **D** Apple and pears with custard

5 Is the statement below TRUE or FALSE?
Charles II marched into England with a Scottish army to reclaim his throne.

- **A** True
- **B** False

6 **A jump jet capable of taking off and landing vertically was developed in the UK. What was it called?**

A The Harrier

B The Kestrel

C The Eagle

D The Bluebird

7 **Is the statement below TRUE or FALSE?**
The Domesday Book no longer exists. It was destroyed at the end of the Norman Conquest.

A True

B False

8 **What are MEPs?**

A Members of the English Parliament

B Members of the European Parliament

C Modern English parliamentarians

D Modern European parliamentarians

9 **Is the statement below TRUE or FALSE?**
The MacDonald clan of Glencoe were massacred.

A True

B False

10 **The First World War ended in victory for Britain and its allies. At what exact time and date in 1918 did the war officially end?**

A 11am on 11 November

B 10am on 10 October

C 6am on 6 June

D 8am on 8 August

11   Is the statement below TRUE or FALSE?
At the beginning of the Middle Ages, England ruled Ireland.

A True

B False

12   Which of the following statements is correct?

A The cabinet's decisions often have to be debated or approved by Parliament.

B The cabinet's decisions must always be debated or approved by Parliament.

13   Who became queen after the death of Edward VI?

A His half-sister Mary

B His wife Mary

C His cousin Mary

D Mary, Queen of Scots

14   Which TWO of the following statements are correct?

A The Romans built roads and public buildings, and created a structure of law.

B The Romans unified the whole of the British Isles.

C The Roman army faced no resistance during the invasions.

D The Romans introduced new plants and animals to Britain.

15   What do you accept and agree to when you become a permanent resident of the UK?

A Catholic beliefs and values

B The right to be tried for crimes in your country of origin

C Traditions of the UK

D Protestant beliefs and values

16 Is the statement below TRUE or FALSE?
The Home Office selects the Police and Crime Commissioners (PCCs).

   A True

   B False

17 When did Queen Victoria's reign end?

   A 1901

   B 1932

   C 1880

   D 1895

18 How is the electoral register updated?

   A Eligible voters must phone their local councillor

   B Every household receives a registration form, which must be completed and returned

   C Every household must request a registration form

   D Every household receives a phone call to enquire about eligible voters

19 In a Crown Court, who decides the verdict of 'guilty' or 'not guilty'?

   A The defendant

   B The barrister

   C The jury

   D The judge

20 The Archbishop of Canterbury can most accurately be described as what?

   A The spiritual leader of the Church of England

   B The political leader of the Church of England

   C The administrative leader of the Church of England

   D The financial leader of the Church of England

21 What were The Canterbury Tales?

- **A** A book of Christian doctrine
- **B** A series of poems
- **C** A Royal Charter
- **D** A story about Canterbury Cathedral

22 Which of the following statements is correct?

- **A** The House of Commons may overrule the House of Lords.
- **B** The House of Commons may never overrule the House of Lords.

23 Which of the following statements about the UK's constitution is not correct?

- **A** The constitution includes laws and conventions.
- **B** The entire constitution is written down in one document.
- **C** The constitution includes the institutions responsible for running the country.
- **D** The constitution includes checks on the power of those who govern the country.

24 Which TWO of the following have the right to vote?

- **A** Adults who have been granted an indefinite right to remain in the UK
- **B** Adults who were born in the UK
- **C** Adults who have been given a visa to study in the UK
- **D** Adults who are naturalised citizens of the UK

ANSWERS: PRACTICE TEST 10

			Handbook reference	Study Guide reference
1	B	South-east Europe	30–1	38–9
2	B	1928	92	100
3	C	15	148	156
4	C	Batter cooked in the oven	108	116
5	A	True	46–8	54–6
6	A	The Harrier	74–5	82–3
7	B	False	33–4	41–2
8	B	Members of the European Parliament	130	138
9	A	True	49–50	57–8
10	A	11am on 11 November	64–5	72–3
11	B	False	35	43
12	A	The cabinet's decisions often have to be debated or approved by Parliament.	131–2	139–40
13	A	His half-sister Mary	40–2	48–50
14	A	The Romans built roads and public buildings, and created a structure of law.	31	39
	D	The Romans introduced new plants and animals to Britain.		
15	C	Traditions of the UK	20–1	28–9
16	B	False	145–6	153–4
17	A	1901	59	67
18	B	Every household receives a registration form, which must be completed and returned	138–9	146–7
19	C	The jury	148–9	156–7
20	A	The spiritual leader of the Church of England	85	93
21	B	A series of poems	37–9	45–7
22	A	The House of Commons may overrule the House of Lords.	129	137
23	B	The entire constitution is written down in one document.	125	133
24	B	Adults who were born in the UK	138	146
	D	Adults who are naturalised citizens of the UK		

PRACTICE TEST 11

1 **Where would the Children's Hearings System deal with cases of children or young people accused of an offence?**

- **A** Northern Ireland
- **B** Wales
- **C** England
- **D** Scotland

2 **Areas of protected countryside that everyone can visit and where people live, work and look after the landscape are called which of the following?**

- **A** Greenfield sites
- **B** Country estates
- **C** National parks
- **D** Moorland

3 **When did Julius Caesar lead the Roman invasion of Britain?**

- **A** 55 BC
- **B** AD 55
- **C** AD 75
- **D** 65 BC

4 **What was the Spanish Armada?**

- **A** A fleet of Spanish ships
- **B** A Spanish princess
- **C** A treaty with Spain
- **D** The Spanish Army

5 **Is the statement below TRUE or FALSE?**
Dame Judi Dench, Colin Firth and Sir Anthony Hopkins have all won film Oscars.

  A True

  B False

6 **The first people lived in Britain during which period?**

  A Ancient times

  B The Jurassic period

  C The Bronze Age

  D The Stone Age

7 **In which language was The Canterbury Tales written?**

  A French

  B Welsh

  C Scottish Gaelic

  D English

8 **In England, parliaments were called when the king needed to consult the nobles and for what other reason?**

  A To lower taxes

  B To create new lords

  C To raise money

  D To call elections

9 **Near which of these cities is Europe's longest dry ski slope?**

  A Aberdeen

  B Inverness

  C Pitlochrie

  D Edinburgh

10 When was the first Union Flag created?

A 1609

B 1606

C 1506

D 1706

11 At the beginning of the 19th century, which one of the following groups could vote?

A All adults over the age of 18

B All women who owned property

C Property-owning men over the age of 21

D Property-owning men over the age of 18

12 Lewis Hamilton is a leading figure in which sport?

A Motor racing

B Horse racing

C Tennis

D Squash

13 Charles II had no legitimate what?

A Right to the throne

B Children

C Government

D Wife

14 Where can HMS Victory be visited?

A Southampton

B Falmouth

C Poole

D Portsmouth

15 The Northern Ireland Assembly makes decisions in which TWO of the following areas?

- **A** Agriculture
- **B** Nuclear energy
- **C** Foreign policy
- **D** The environment

16 Which TWO places did the Vikings come from?

- **A** Belgium
- **B** France
- **C** Denmark
- **D** Norway

17 Which TWO facts are true of the individual registration system?

- **A** Registered voters remain on the register until a change in their personal details
- **B** Eligible voters complete their own voter registration forms
- **C** An individual registers his or her whole family to vote
- **D** The electoral register is fully updated each year

18 What did Iron Age people sometimes defend?

- **A** Hill forts
- **B** Castles
- **C** Long walls
- **D** None of the above

19 Which of the following statements is correct?

- **A** You should always introduce yourself to your neighbours when you move into a new house or flat.
- **B** You should never introduce yourself to your new neighbours, but should let them introduce themselves.

20 **When did Parliament as we know it today begin to develop?**

- **A** The Iron Age
- **B** The Stone Age
- **C** The Middle Ages
- **D** The Bronze Age

21 **Which TWO actions can political parties undertake to gain support for their candidate?**

- **A** Threatening people to make them vote a certain way
- **B** Handing out leaflets
- **C** Knocking on doors and talking to people about their candidate
- **D** Paying people to vote a certain way

22 **In the 19th century, the UK became a centre for services such as banking and insurance. What sector of the economy do these services belong to?**

- **A** Finance
- **B** Agriculture
- **C** Manufacturing
- **D** Entertainment

23 **Is the statement below TRUE or FALSE?**
ISAF is building up the Afghan National Security Forces and helping to create a secure environment in which governance and development can be extended.

- **A** True
- **B** False

24 **What title did Napoleon take?**

- **A** King
- **B** Naval Commander
- **C** Emperor
- **D** Lord Admiral

ANSWERS: PRACTICE TEST 11

			Handbook reference	Study Guide reference
1	D	Scotland	149	157
2	C	National parks	112	120
3	A	55 BC	31	39
4	A	A fleet of Spanish ships	43–4	51–2
5	A	True	108–9	116–7
6	D	The Stone Age	30–1	38–9
7	D	English	37–9	45–7
8	C	To raise money	36–7	44–5
9	D	Edinburgh	96	104
10	B	1606	58	66
11	C	Property-owning men over the age of 21	124	132
12	A	Motor racing	96	104
13	B	Children	49	57
14	D	Portsmouth	56–7	64–5
15	A	Agriculture	133–7	141–5
	D	The environment		
16	C	Denmark	33	41
	D	Norway		
17	A	Registered voters remain on the register until a change in their personal details	138–9	146–7
	B	Eligible voters complete their own voter registration forms		
18	A	Hill forts	30–1	38–9
19	A	You should always introduce yourself to your neighbours when you move into a new house or flat.	159	167
20	C	The Middle Ages	36–7	44–5
21	B	Handing out leaflets	161	169
	C	Knocking on doors and talking to people about their candidate		
22	A	Finance	59–60	67–8
23	A	True	77–8	85–6
24	C	Emperor	56–7	64–5

PRACTICE TEST 12

1   Who was William Shakespeare?

- **A** A naval commander
- **B** A Scottish patriot
- **C** An English parliamentarian
- **D** A poet, actor and playwright

2   A delay in introducing Home Rule to Ireland resulted in the Easter uprising, which took place in which city?

- **A** Belfast
- **B** Dublin
- **C** Cork
- **D** London

3   Charles I believed in, and tried to rule in line with, what principle?

- **A** Democracy
- **B** Primogeniture
- **C** Religious virtue
- **D** The Divine Right of Kings

4   Who is the heir to the throne?

- **A** Prince Philip
- **B** Prince Charles
- **C** The Prime Minister
- **D** All of the above

5   Which of the following statements is correct?

- **A** More than 190 countries belong to NATO.
- **B** More than 190 countries belong to the United Nations.

6 During the First World War the British fought against countries including Germany, the Ottoman Empire and the Austro-Hungarian Empire. What was this alliance known as?

- **A** The Middle Powers
- **B** The Central Powers
- **C** The Germanic Powers
- **D** The Autocratic Powers

7 Is the statement below TRUE or FALSE?
Breaking a Forced Marriage Protection Order can result in a prison sentence.

- **A** True
- **B** False

8 What is the capital city of Wales?

- **A** Newport
- **B** Cardiff
- **C** Swansea
- **D** Plymouth

9 When did the first farmers come to Britain?

- **A** 10,000 years ago
- **B** 3,000 years ago
- **C** 6,000 years ago
- **D** 8,000 years ago

10 Is the statement below TRUE or FALSE?
During the Industrial Revolution, canals were built to link factories to cities, towns and ports, particularly in the middle and north of England.

- **A** True
- **B** False

11 Who could not get Parliament to agree to his or her religious and foreign policy views and tried to rule without Parliament?

- **A** Charles I
- **B** Elizabeth I
- **C** Bloody Mary
- **D** Henry VIII

12 In the UK, it is acceptable to discriminate against people for which of the following?

- **A** Age
- **B** Religion or beliefs
- **C** Pregnancy or maternity
- **D** None of the above

13 During the reign of which king of England was the Domesday Book compiled?

- **A** Harold
- **B** William the Conqueror
- **C** Kenneth MacAlpin
- **D** Alfred the Great

14 Which TWO of the following deal with civil disputes?

- **A** Sheriff Court
- **B** Crown Court
- **C** County Court
- **D** Youth Court

15 Which of the following is not a core value of the civil service?

- **A** Honesty
- **B** Party loyalty
- **C** Integrity
- **D** Objectivity

16 Which TWO of the following are offences?

A Driving without motor insurance

B Failing to have an MOT certificate for a car under three years old

C Failing to have an AA or RAC membership

D Driving a car that is more than three years old and does not have an MOT certificate

17 Was King Henry I on the throne at the time of the Magna Carta?

A Yes

B No

18 Who was Kenneth MacAlpin?

A A Danish king

B An Anglo-Saxon king

C A Scottish king

D A Viking

19 How large is Loch Lomond and The Trossachs National Park?

A 560 square miles or 1,451 square kilometres

B 1,580 square miles or 4,093 square kilometres

C 720 square miles or 1,865 square kilometres

D 1,865 square miles or 720 square kilometres

20 A poll card includes which TWO pieces of information?

A The date of the election

B Who you should vote for

C Where the polling station or polling place is located

D How much tax you should pay

21 **West Germany, France, Luxembourg, the Netherlands and Italy formed the European Economic Community (EEC) in 1957 along with which other country?**

A Ireland

B Belgium

C Sweden

D Albania

22 **In Northern Ireland, children who have committed an offence are dealt with by which of the following?**

A A Sheriff Court

B A Crown Court

C The Children's Hearings System

D A system of youth conferencing

23 **The first day of one notorious battle in 1916 resulted in 60,000 British casualties. What was this battle?**

A The Battle of the Somme

B The Battle of the Bulge

C The Battle of Agincourt

D The Battle of the River Plate

24 **What happened to Catherine Parr soon after she remarried, following the death of Henry VIII?**

A She had a son

B She died

C She had a daughter

D She was executed

ANSWERS: PRACTICE TEST 12

			Handbook reference	Study Guide reference
1	D	A poet, actor and playwright	44	52
2	B	Dublin	65–6	73–4
3	D	The Divine Right of Kings	45–6	53–4
4	B	Prince Charles	125–7	133–5
5	B	More than 190 countries belong to the United Nations.	143	151
6	B	The Central Powers	64–5	72–3
7	A	True	155	163
8	B	Cardiff	81	89
9	C	6,000 years ago	30–1	38–9
10	A	True	53–5	61–3
11	A	Charles I	45–6	53–4
12	D	None of the above	154	162
13	B	William the Conqueror	33–4	41–2
14	A	Sheriff Court	151–3	159–61
	C	County Court		
15	B	Party loyalty	133	141
16	A	Driving without motor insurance	157	165
	D	Driving a car that is more than three years old and does not have an MOT certificate		
17	B	No	36	44
18	C	A Scottish king	33	41
19	C	720 square miles or 1,865 square kilometres	117	125
20	A	The date of the election	139	147
	C	Where the polling station or polling place is located		
21	B	Belgium	76	84
22	D	A system of youth conferencing	149	157
23	A	The Battle of the Somme	64–5	72–3
24	B	She died	41	49

PRACTICE TEST 13

1 **Is the statement below TRUE or FALSE?**
Following the abolition of slavery, two million Chinese and
Indian workers were employed to replace the freed slaves.

A True

B False

2 **With the exception of Scotland, a jury has how many members?**

A 10

B 12

C 15

D 20

3 **Mary Stuart, the queen of Scotland was often**
known by which other name?

A Mary Tudor

B Blood Mary

C Mary, Queen of Scotland

D Mary, Queen of Scots

4 **Gertrude Jekyll is famous for her designs in which field?**

A Fashion

B Gardening

C Silverware

D Pottery

5 **Which of these statements about Roald Dahl is not true?**

A He began to publish books and short stories in the 1940s.

B He served in the Royal Air Force during the Second World War.

C He had Norwegian parents.

D He served in the Royal Navy during the Second World War.

6   Which of the following statements is correct?

A In Scotland, serious offences are tried in a Sheriff Court.

B In Scotland, serious offences are tried in a Crown Court.

7   During 1940, German troops defeated allied forces whilst advancing through which country?

A Russia

B France

C Greece

D Argentina

8   In which TWO places are arrangements different for taking your Life in the UK test?

A Scotland

B Ireland

C Isle of Man

D Channel Islands

9   Which of the following was a co-discoverer of insulin?

A John Logie Baird

B Sir Frank Whittle

C John MacLeod

D Sir Robert Watson-Watt

10 Is the statement below TRUE or FALSE?
The whole British Empire was involved in the First World War, with troops from India, the West Indies, Africa, and Australia all fighting on behalf of the British.

A True

B False

11 **The Victorian period famously saw reformers leading moves to improve conditions for which section of society?**

A The aristocracy

B The poor

C The middle classes

D The clergy

12 **In which year of the reign of Charles II was there a major outbreak of plague?**

A 1625

B 1645

C 1695

D 1665

13 **What were women campaigning for the right to vote known as?**

A Suffragettes

B Votettes

C Democrettes

D Feminettes

14 **In Scotland, the legal system developed differently from the one in England in that its laws were 'codified'. What is meant by codified?**

A Less complicated

B Dictated by Parliament

C Written down

D Based on tradition

15 **Is the statement below TRUE or FALSE?**
Charles I was interested in science. During his reign, the 'Royal Society' was formed.

A True

B False

16 Which TWO of these careers did Winston Churchill follow before becoming a Conservative MP in 1900?

- **A** Teacher
- **B** Vicar
- **C** Journalist
- **D** Soldier

17 What did the missionaries teach the Anglo-Saxons?

- **A** About other cultures
- **B** About Christianity
- **C** About other languages
- **D** About trade

18 Why were James I and Charles I less skilled at managing Parliament than Elizabeth I?

- **A** They didn't want to get involved in the democratic process and left decision-making to advisors
- **B** They believed in the 'Divine Right of Kings' to make decisions without the approval of Parliament
- **C** They misjudged the changing nature of parliamentary democracy
- **D** They were undermined by extreme opposition to their views and gave up

19 In which year did the Wars of the Roses begin?

- **A** 1455
- **B** 1560
- **C** 1425
- **D** 1535

20 Who wrote Paradise Lost?

- **A** William Shakespeare
- **B** Salman Rushdie
- **C** Rider Haggard
- **D** John Milton

21 The Festival of Lights is a non-Christian festival known as which of the following?

- **A** Vaisakhi
- **B** Hannukah
- **C** Diwali
- **D** Eid ul Adha

22 Who gave the throne to her Protestant son, James VI?

- **A** Elizabeth I
- **B** Mary Tudor
- **C** Mary, Queen of Scots
- **D** Bloody Mary

23 The game of golf is traditionally thought to have originated in which country?

- **A** England
- **B** Spain
- **C** USA
- **D** Scotland

24 What did Sir Edmond Halley predict?

- **A** The return of a comet
- **B** The restoration of the monarchy
- **C** The defeat of the Spanish Armada
- **D** The Great Fire of London

ANSWERS: PRACTICE TEST 13

			Handbook reference	Study Guide reference
1	A	True	55–6	63–4
2	B	12	148–9	156–7
3	D	Mary, Queen of Scots	43	51
4	B	Gardening	102–3	110–1
5	D	He served in the Royal Navy during the Second World War.	77	85
6	A	In Scotland, serious offences are tried in a Sheriff Court.	148	156
7	B	France	66–9	74–7
8	C	Isle of Man	22–3	30–1
	D	Channel Islands		
9	C	John MacLeod	74–5	82–3
10	A	True	64–5	72–3
11	B	The poor	59	67
12	D	1665	48	56
13	A	Suffragettes	61–2	69–70
14	C	Written down	36–7	44–5
15	B	False	48	56
16	C	Journalist	68	76
	D	Soldier		
17	B	About Christianity	31–3	39–41
18	B	They believed in the 'Divine Right of Kings' to make decisions without the approval of Parliament	45–6	53–4
19	A	1455	39	47
20	D	John Milton	104–6	112–4
21	C	Diwali	88	96
22	C	Mary, Queen of Scots	43	51
23	D	Scotland	95	103
24	A	The return of a comet	48	56

PRACTICE TEST 14

1 Which one of the following is not a benefit of volunteering?

- **A** Being able to add new experience to your CV
- **B** Being paid
- **C** Having a chance to practise English
- **D** Meeting new people

2 What did hereditary peers lose in 1999?

- **A** The right to own land
- **B** The automatic right to sit in the House of Lords
- **C** The right to elect other peers to the House of Lords
- **D** The right to speak in Parliament

3 Jane Seymour gave birth to the son Henry VIII wanted. What was his name?

- **A** Henry
- **B** Edmund
- **C** Edward
- **D** Richard

4 What can people who are unable to go to a polling place or polling station register to receive?

- **A** A postal ballot
- **B** An absentee ballot
- **C** An absentee vote
- **D** A virtual ballot

5 **All terrorist groups try to get people to join them. What is this activity called?**

- **A** Education
- **B** Recruitment
- **C** Conversation
- **D** Kidnapping

6 **Is this statement TRUE or FALSE?**
During Queen Victoria's reign the French Empire became the largest Empire the world has ever seen.

- **A** True
- **B** False

7 **Who decides what should happen in legal disputes over contracts, property rights or employment rights?**

- **A** The media
- **B** The police
- **C** The judiciary
- **D** The peers

8 **During the 18th century, Britain fought a number of wars with which country?**

- **A** India
- **B** South Africa
- **C** Spain
- **D** France

9 **Which of the following statements is correct?**

- **A** The National Assembly for Wales and the Welsh government are based in Edinburgh.
- **B** The National Assembly for Wales and the Welsh government are based in Cardiff.

10   Which of the following statements is correct?

   A   The Commonwealth is a group of countries that support each other and work together.

   B   The Commonwealth is a group of regions that together make up a federal republic.

11   Which TWO of these races did Mo Farah win in the 2012 London Olympics?

   A   5,000 metres

   B   10,000 metres

   C   3,000 metre steeplechase

   D   Marathon

12   What sorts of stories were depicted in the stained glass windows of many cathedrals built in the Middle Ages?

   A   Stories about kings and coronations

   B   Stories about battles and victories

   C   Stories about the Bible and saints

   D   Stories about communities and farming

13   Is the statement below TRUE or FALSE?
St Columba became the first Archbishop of Canterbury.

   A   True

   B   False

14   Is the statement below TRUE or FALSE?
Sake Dean Mahomet was born in 1759 and grew up in the Bengal region of India.

   A   True

   B   False

15 **Which of these countries was part of the British Empire during Victoria's reign?**

- **A** France
- **B** Switzerland
- **C** USA
- **D** India

16 **Which organisation was founded in 1895 and now has over 61,000 volunteers helping to preserve important buildings, the countryside and the coastline?**

- **A** The National Trust
- **B** The Countryside Alliance
- **C** Country Landowners Association
- **D** The National Gardens Scheme

17 **Which of the following statements is correct?**

- **A** In 1789 there was an unpopular new government in France and Britain declared war.
- **B** In 1789 there was a revolution in France and the new French government declared war on Britain.

18 **During the reign of Henry VII what happened to the power of the nobility in England?**

- **A** It was reduced
- **B** It increased
- **C** It was abolished
- **D** It was absolute

19 **Is the statement below TRUE or FALSE?**
The Old Bailey is the world's most famous Magistrates' Court.

- **A** True
- **B** False

20 **During the 19th century, Britain and the East India Company gained control of large parts of which TWO countries?**

- **A** The United States
- **B** Canada
- **C** India
- **D** Singapore

21 **Why was the English victory at the Battle of Agincourt unexpected?**

- **A** King Henry V was killed
- **B** The English army had fewer weapons
- **C** The English army was weakened by illness
- **D** The French army outnumbered the English

22 **Briton Sir Tim Berners-Lee invented the World Wide Web and information was successfully transferred via the web for the first time on 25 December 1990.**

- **A** True
- **B** False

23 **Is the statement below TRUE or FALSE?**
Britain had colonies in southern Africa in the 19th century.

- **A** True
- **B** False

24 **Which famous religious building has been the coronation church since 1066 and is the final resting place for 17 monarchs?**

- **A** Westminster Abbey
- **B** York Minster
- **C** St Paul's Cathedral
- **D** Westminster Cathedral

ANSWERS: PRACTICE TEST 14

			Handbook reference	Study Guide reference
1	B	Being paid	162–4	170–2
2	B	The automatic right to sit in the House of Lords	129	137
3	C	Edward	40–2	48–50
4	A	A postal ballot	139	147
5	B	Recruitment	147	155
6	B	False	59	67
7	C	The judiciary	148–9	156–7
8	D	France	56–7	64–5
9	B	The National Assembly for Wales and the Welsh government are based in Cardiff.	133–7	141–5
10	A	The Commonwealth is a group of countries that support each other and work together.	141	149
11	A	5,000 metres	92–3	100–1
	B	10,000 metres		
12	C	Stories about the Bible and saints	37–9	45–7
13	B	False	31–3	39–41
14	A	True	55	63
15	D	India	59	67
16	A	The National Trust	112	120
17	B	In 1789 there was a revolution in France and the new French government declared war on Britain.	56–7	64–5
18	A	It was reduced	40–2	48–50
19	B	False	149	157
20	B	Canada	53–5	61–3
	C	India		
21	D	The French army outnumbered the English	35	43
22	A	True	74–5	82–3
23	A	True	53–5	61–3
24	A	Westminster Abbey	86	94

PRACTICE TEST 15

1 During the 19th century, which sector of the Irish economy supported around two-thirds of its people?

A Tourism

B Farming

C Manufacturing

D Shipbuilding

2 What do we know about the life of Anne Boleyn?

A She had one daughter with Henry VIII named Elizabeth

B She died shortly after giving birth

C She married Henry VIII late in his life, and survived him

D She ruled with William III after the Glorious Revolution

3 What was needed during the Industrial Revolution to power the new factories?

A Coal

B Slaves

C Oil

D Looms

4 The official title of the famous Beveridge Report of 1942 was what?

A Social Insurance and Allied Services

B The Fight Against Want, Disease, Ignorance, Squalor and Idleness

C A Basis for the Modern Welfare State

D Poverty and How to Solve it

5 **By 1200, the English ruled an area of Ireland around Dublin known as what?**

- **A** The Pate
- **B** The Pict
- **C** The Pale
- **D** The Plain

6 **Official reports of parliamentary proceeding are published in which of the following?**

- **A** The BBC magazine
- **B** Hansard
- **C** The Telegraph
- **D** The Sunday Times

7 **Which of these sectors was not nationalised by the post-war Labour government?**

- **A** Coal mining
- **B** The railways
- **C** Gas, electric and water supplies
- **D** Farming

8 **James II invaded Ireland in an attempt to regain the throne with an army from which country?**

- **A** Germany
- **B** France
- **C** Scotland
- **D** Wales

9   Following the introduction of the Bill of Rights, monarchs were required to ask Parliament to renew funding for which TWO of the following each year?

- **A** Army
- **B** Building of castles
- **C** Palaces
- **D** Navy

10   Why were more castles built in Britain and Ireland in the Middle Ages?

- **A** They were cheap to build
- **B** They were defensive strongholds
- **C** They were status symbols for the nobility
- **D** They created work for tradesmen

11   Which of these statements is correct?

- **A** You will need the help of a lawyer to issue a small claim.
- **B** You do not need the help of a lawyer to issue a small claim.

12   Which of the following statements is correct?

- **A** 11 November commemorates soldiers who died in World War One but it also remembers those who have died in all conflicts involving the UK since then.
- **B** 11 November commemorates soldiers who died in World War One and a separate date in the year is set aside to commemorate the end of the Second World War in 1945.

13   Is this statement TRUE or FALSE?
In Wales and Northern Ireland the established Churches are respectively the Church of Wales and the Church of Ulster.

- **A** True
- **B** False

14 **In which year did the BBC begin the world's
first regular television service?**

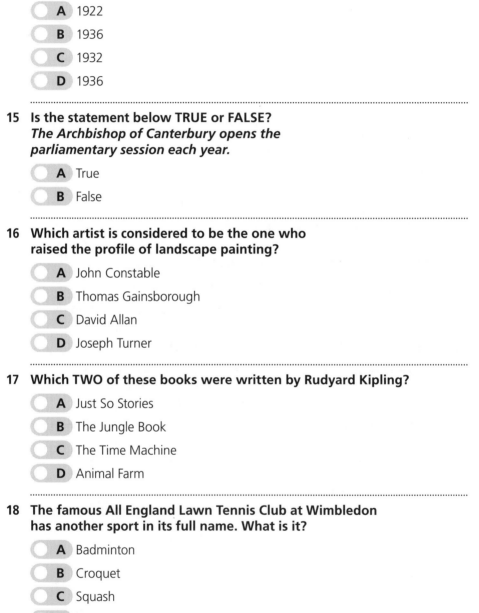

- **A** 1922
- **B** 1936
- **C** 1932
- **D** 1936

15 **Is the statement below TRUE or FALSE?**
*The Archbishop of Canterbury opens the
parliamentary session each year.*

- **A** True
- **B** False

16 **Which artist is considered to be the one who
raised the profile of landscape painting?**

- **A** John Constable
- **B** Thomas Gainsborough
- **C** David Allan
- **D** Joseph Turner

17 **Which TWO of these books were written by Rudyard Kipling?**

- **A** Just So Stories
- **B** The Jungle Book
- **C** The Time Machine
- **D** Animal Farm

18 **The famous All England Lawn Tennis Club at Wimbledon
has another sport in its full name. What is it?**

- **A** Badminton
- **B** Croquet
- **C** Squash
- **D** Rackets

19 Which of these statements about Margaret Thatcher is not true?

   A She became a cabinet minister in 1970

   B Her first job in the cabinet was as Secretary
of State for Education and Science

   C Her second cabinet position was Chancellor of the Exchequer

   D She was elected as leader of the Conservative Party,
and thus leader of the opposition, in 1975

**20 What happened when Charles I tried to impose a revised
Prayer Book onto the Presbyterian Church in Scotland?**

   A There was serious unrest

   B It was very popular

   C It was accepted with a few amendments

   D Charles was beheaded

**21 Can young people in every part of the UK volunteer
with the National Citizen Service?**

   A Yes, but each part of the UK has a different
website for information about the service

   B No, only young people resident in England can volunteer

22 Which of these statements is not correct?

   A St George is the patron saint of England.

   B St Andrew is the patron saint of Scotland.

   C St David is the patron saint of Wales.

   D St Paul is the patron saint of Ireland.

23 **The British government wanted to tax the North American colonies, which were wealthy and largely controlled their own affairs. What TWO impacts did this have?**

A   It was seen by colonists as an attack on freedom

B   Colonists accepted taxation and were loyal to the crown

C   Colonists wanted representation in Parliament if they were to be taxed

D   Colonists wanted Parliament to tax only certain people

24 **Which of the following countries does not belong to the Commonwealth?**

A   Canada

B   Germany

C   Ghana

D   Singapore

ANSWERS: PRACTICE TEST 15

			Handbook reference	Study Guide reference
1	B	Farming	61	69
2	A	She had one daughter with Henry VIII named Elizabeth	40–2	48–50
3	A	Coal	53–5	61–3
4	A	Social Insurance and Allied Services	71	79
5	C	The Pale	35	43
6	B	Hansard	137	145
7	D	Farming	70–1	78–9
8	B	France	49–50	57–8
9	A	Army	51	59
	D	Navy		
10	B	They were defensive strongholds	37–9	45–7
11	B	You do not need the help of a lawyer to issue a small claim.	151	159
12	A	11 November commemorates soldiers who died in World War One but it also remembers those who have died in all conflicts involving the UK since then.	90	98
13	B	False	85	93
14	D	1936	66	74
15	B	False	125–7	133–5
16	D	Joseph Turner	101	109
17	A	Just So Stories	63	71
	B	The Jungle Book		
18	B	Croquet	96	104
19	C	Her second cabinet position was Chancellor of the Exchequer	76	84
20	A	There was serious unrest	46	54
21	A	Yes, but each part of the UK has a different website for information about the service	162–4	170–2
22	D	St Paul is the patron saint of Ireland.	85–6	93–4
23	A	It was seen by colonists as an attack on freedom	56	64
	C	Colonists wanted representation in Parliament if they were to be taxed		
24	B	Germany	141–2	149–50

PRACTICE TEST 16

1   Some people in Britain were opposed to the slave trade. Who set up the first formal anti-slavery groups in the late 1700s?

   A Methodists

   B Mormons

   C Quakers

   D Puritans

2   What is the capital city of Scotland?

   A Edinburgh

   B Glasgow

   C Dundee

   D Aberdeen

3   The Elizabethan period in England was a time of growing patriotism. What do we mean by this?

   A There was unrest and instability

   B The monarchy became unpopular

   C The country became more democratic

   D A feeling of pride in being English

4   On which day do people send cards to someone they admire, anonymously?

   A Christmas Day

   B New Year's Day

   C Valentine's Day

   D April Fool's Day

5 **Where do solicitors often advertise their services?**

   A Yellow Pages

   B On Crown Court notice boards

   C On the BBC

   D All of the above

6 **How many countries belong to the Commonwealth?**

   A 12

   B 25

   C 39

   D 54

7 **Which of the following statements is correct?**

   A During the Elizabethan period, English settlers began to colonise the eastern coast of America.

   B During the Elizabethan period, English settlers began to colonise the western coast of America.

8 **Which of the following is not a document setting out rights or freedoms?**

   A The UK Constitution

   B The Habeas Corpus Act

   C The Magna Carta

   D The Bill of Rights of 1689

9 **Is the statement below TRUE or FALSE?**
Henry VIII continued his father's work to centralise the administrative powers of England.

   A True

   B False

10 In which part of the UK was pioneering doctor Alexander Fleming born in 1881?

- **A** Wales
- **B** Scotland
- **C** East Anglia
- **D** Cornwall

11 Which of these statements about the British Empire in the Victorian period is true?

- **A** At its peak, the Empire had an estimated population of just under 400 million.
- **B** The Empire included half the countries of Europe.
- **C** The Empire did not extend into Africa.
- **D** Half of Australia was part of the British Empire and half was part of the French Empire.

12 In 1913, the British government promised Home Rule for Ireland. Which group within Ireland threatened to resist this move by force?

- **A** The Protestants in the south
- **B** The Muslims in the east
- **C** The Buddhists in the west
- **D** The Protestants in the north

13 Which TWO of the following happened when William of Orange invaded England in 1688?

- **A** James II fled to France
- **B** There was a battle in which James II was killed
- **C** William became William III and reigned jointly with his wife Mary
- **D** William was attacked in the English Channel and his ship sank

14 Is the statement below TRUE or FALSE?
All MPs represent one of the main political parties.

- **A** True
- **B** False

15 Who were the Picts?

- **A** Ancestors of the Irish people
- **B** Ancestors of the Welsh people
- **C** Ancestors of the Scottish people
- **D** Ancestors of the English people

16 What are biomes, which are found at the Eden Project?

- **A** Large South American plants
- **B** Large greenhouses
- **C** Picnic areas
- **D** Automatic watering mechanisms

17 During the English Civil War, in which TWO battles was Charles I's army defeated?

- **A** Battle of Bosworth Field
- **B** Battle of Naseby
- **C** Battle of Marston Moor
- **D** Battle of Hastings

18 Why did Henry VIII marry Anne of Cleves?

- **A** For political reasons
- **B** He loved her
- **C** To have a male heir
- **D** She was beautiful

19 **Anyone who wishes to buy tobacco or tobacco products must be over what age?**

- **A** 14
- **B** 16
- **C** 18
- **D** 21

20 **Which Northern Irish portrait artist, who died in 1941, painted some portraits of the Royal Family?**

- **A** Sir John Lavery
- **B** Paul Henry
- **C** Basil Blackshaw
- **D** Markey Robinson

21 **When the monarchy was restored, Charles II was crowned king of which countries?**

- **A** England, Wales and Ireland
- **B** England, Wales, Scotland and Ireland
- **C** England, Scotland and Wales
- **D** England and Wales

22 **After Protestants, which is the biggest denomination of Christianity in the UK?**

- **A** Jehovah's Witnesses
- **B** Roman Catholic
- **C** Ethiopian Orthodox
- **D** Christian Science

23 Who introduced a system called feudalism to Britain?

- **A** Vikings
- **B** Jutes
- **C** Normans
- **D** Anglo-Saxons

24 Pumpkins, lit with candles, are used to celebrate which tradition?

- **A** Bonfire Night
- **B** Halloween
- **C** Midsummer
- **D** May Day

ANSWERS: PRACTICE TEST 16

			Handbook reference	Study Guide reference
1	C	Quakers	55–6	63–4
2	A	Edinburgh	81	89
3	D	A feeling of pride in being English.	43–4	51–2
4	C	Valentine's Day	90	98
5	A	Yellow Pages	152–3	160–1
6	D	54	141	149
7	A	During the Elizabethan period, English settlers began to colonise the eastern coast of America.	43–4	51–2
8	A	The UK Constitution	153–4	161–2
9	A	True	40–2	48–50
10	B	Scotland	70	78
11	A	At its peak, the Empire had an estimated population of just under 400 million.	59	67
12	D	The Protestants in the north	65–6	73–4
13	A	James II fled to France	49–50	57–8
	C	William became William III and reigned jointly with his wife Mary		
14	B	False	132	140
15	C	Ancestors of the Scottish people	31	39
16	B	Large greenhouses	114	122
17	B	Battle of Naseby	46–8	54–6
	C	Battle of Marston Moor		
18	A	For political reasons	41	49
19	C	18	144–5	152–3
20	A	Sir John Lavery	101	109
21	B	England, Wales, Scotland and Ireland	48	56
22	B	Roman Catholic	85	93
23	C	Normans	35–6	43–4
24	B	Halloween	90	98

PRACTICE TEST 17

1 When William of Orange came to the throne with his wife Mary, this later became known as the Glorious Revolution. Why?

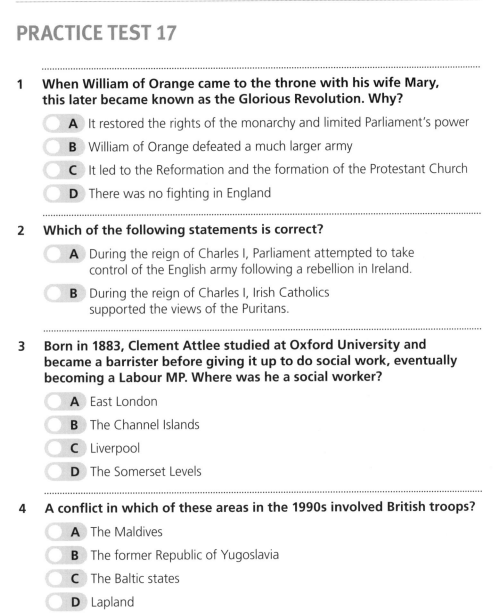

A It restored the rights of the monarchy and limited Parliament's power

B William of Orange defeated a much larger army

C It led to the Reformation and the formation of the Protestant Church

D There was no fighting in England

2 Which of the following statements is correct?

A During the reign of Charles I, Parliament attempted to take control of the English army following a rebellion in Ireland.

B During the reign of Charles I, Irish Catholics supported the views of the Puritans.

3 Born in 1883, Clement Attlee studied at Oxford University and became a barrister before giving it up to do social work, eventually becoming a Labour MP. Where was he a social worker?

A East London

B The Channel Islands

C Liverpool

D The Somerset Levels

4 A conflict in which of these areas in the 1990s involved British troops?

A The Maldives

B The former Republic of Yugoslavia

C The Baltic states

D Lapland

5 Is the statement below TRUE or FALSE?
There are no differences between the court systems of England, Northern Ireland, Scotland and Wales.

A True

B False

6 Which TWO of the following statements about the Norman invasion are correct?

A The Norman invasion of England was unsuccessful.

B The Norman conquest led to changes in government and social structures in England.

C The Norman conquest was the last successful foreign invasion of England.

D The Norman conquest had very little influence on Anglo-Saxon life.

7 Which of the following statements regarding the British Empire is not true?

A The Empire continued to expand into the 1920s.

B From the late 19th century, there was discussion about the future of Empire, with many believing it should expand and others seeing its size as a drain on resources.

C At the start of the 20th century, the vast majority of British people still saw the Empire as a force for good in the world.

D In 1910 the British and Spanish Empires merged.

8 Is the statement below TRUE or FALSE?
Protestants believed that a person's own relationship with God was more important than submitting to the authority of the Church.

A True

B False

9 Which of the following statements is correct?

A Completed ballots must be handed to an election official.

B Completed ballots must be placed in a ballot box.

10 In which decade was the jet engine developed by Sir Frank Whittle, a British Royal Air Force engineer officer?

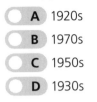

- **A** 1920s
- **B** 1970s
- **C** 1950s
- **D** 1930s

11 Is the statement below TRUE or FALSE?
In the UK, everybody has the right to choose their religion or choose not to practise a religion – in the 2009 Citizenship Survey, 21% of people said they followed no religion.

- **A** True
- **B** False

12 Is the statement below TRUE or FALSE?
The language of the Iron Age was part of the Celtic language family and related languages are still spoken today in parts of Scotland, Wales and Ireland.

- **A** True
- **B** False

13 When England became a republic it no longer had what?

- **A** Parliament
- **B** National anthem
- **C** Monarch
- **D** Prime Minister

14 Is the statement below TRUE or FALSE?
In 1690, following his unsuccessful attempt to regain his throne in Ireland, James II fled back to the Netherlands.

- **A** True
- **B** False

15 Income tax is not paid on which of the following forms of income?

A Pension

B Money you win on the lottery

C Benefits

D All of the above

16 Small claims procedures can be used for which TWO of the following?

A Any claim below £10,000 in England and Wales

B Any claim below £5,000 in Scotland and Northern Ireland

C Any claim below £5,000 in England and Wales

D Any claim below £3,000 in Scotland and Northern Ireland

17 What was the Turing machine, invented by Alan Turing?

A A theoretical mathematical device that was influential in the development of computer science and the modern-day computer

B A car that ran on water

C A high-speed photocopier that revolutionised office work

D An innovative vacuum cleaner that was sold across the world

18 Is the statement below TRUE or FALSE?
It is possible to find information about visiting Parliament on the UK Parliament website.

A True

B False

19 Is the statement below TRUE or FALSE?
The Houses of Parliament are built in the medieval 'gothic' style of architecture.

A True

B False

20 The Elizabeth Tower is part of which building in London?

- **A** St Paul's Cathedral
- **B** Houses of Parliament
- **C** Mansion House
- **D** Buckingham Palace

21 Is it possible for the leader of the opposition to become Prime Minister?

- **A** Yes, if the Prime Minister resigns
- **B** Yes, if his or her party wins a General Election

22 People usually spend Christmas Day at home and enjoy a special meal that normally includes Christmas pudding, mince pies and which meat?

- **A** Duck
- **B** Turkey
- **C** Guinea fowl
- **D** Pork

23 Which TWO of the following describe the purpose of the UN Security Council?

- **A** To promote human rights
- **B** To recommend action during an international crisis
- **C** To recommend action where there is a threat to peace
- **D** To make international law

24 Which of the following is the title of the David Lean directed film of 1962?

- **A** Lawrence of Asia
- **B** Lawrence of Australia
- **C** Lawrence of Amsterdam
- **D** Lawrence of Arabia

LIFE IN THE UK TEST: PRACTICE QUESTIONS

ANSWERS: PRACTICE TEST 17

			Handbook reference	Study Guide reference
1	D	There was no fighting in England	49–50	57–8
2	A	During the reign of Charles I, Parliament attempted to take control of the English army following a rebellion in Ireland.	46	54
3	A	East London	71	79
4	B	The former Republic of Yugoslavia	77–8	85–6
5	B	False	148–9	156–7
6	B	The Norman conquest led to changes in government and social structures in England.	33–4	41–2
	C	The Norman conquest was the last successful foreign invasion of England.		
7	D	In 1910 the British and Spanish Empires merged.	63	71
8	A	True	40–2	48–50
9	B	Completed ballots must be placed in a ballot box.	139	147
10	D	1930s	74–5	82–3
11	A	True	84	92
12	A	True	30–1	38–9
13	C	Monarch	46–8	54–6
14	B	False	49–50	57–8
15	B	Money you win on the lottery	155–6	163–4
16	C	Any claim below £5,000 in England and Wales	151	159
	D	Any claim below £3,000 in Scotland and Northern Ireland		
17	A	A theoretical mathematical device that was influential in the development of computer science and the modern-day computer	74–5	82–3
18	A	True	140–1	148–9
19	A	True	102–3	110–1
20	B	Houses of Parliament	113	121
21	B	Yes, if his or her party wins a General Election	132	140
22	B	Turkey	87	95
23	B	To recommend action during an international crisis	143	151
	C	To recommend action where there is a threat to peace		
24	D	Lawrence of Arabia	109	117

PRACTICE TEST 18: SCOTLAND

1 **Police forces are headed by whom?**

- **A** Ministers
- **B** Generals
- **C** Mayors
- **D** Chief Constables

2 **Is the statement below TRUE or FALSE?**
A Formula 1 Grand Prix race is held in Britain every year.

- **A** True
- **B** False

3 **Is the statement below TRUE or FALSE?**
Many colonists had gone to North America in order to have religious freedom.

- **A** True
- **B** False

4 **During the 1960s, Parliament passed new laws that made it illegal for employers to discriminate against women because of their gender and gave them which right?**

- **A** Free lunches
- **B** Equal pay
- **C** Childcare at work
- **D** Two years' maternity leave

5 **Which of the following is the title of a piece of music written by Sir William Walton?**

- **A** Balthazar's Festival
- **B** Balthazar's Funeral
- **C** Balthazar's Feast
- **D** Balthazar's Fellowship

6 Serious unrest in Northern Ireland in the 1970s led to what event happening in 1972?

- **A** The Irish army invaded Northern Ireland.
- **B** A multinational United Nations force occupied Northern Ireland.
- **C** The Northern Ireland Parliament was suspended and direct rule from the UK was re-introduced.
- **D** Seaports and airports were blocked to prevent suspected terrorists leaving the country.

7 The UK joined the EEC in which year?

- **A** 1945
- **B** 1957
- **C** 1973
- **D** 2000

8 Mary Stuart was forced to flee England after being accused of murder. Who was she accused of murdering?

- **A** Her father
- **B** Her husband
- **C** Her brother
- **D** Her sister

9 Which of these countries did not fight on the side of the Allied Powers during the First World War?

- **A** Bulgaria
- **B** Italy
- **C** USA
- **D** Serbia

10 **King Edward I of England annexed Wales to the crown of England by which statute?**

  A The Statute of Caernarfon

  B The Statute of Gwynedd

  C The Statute of Carmarthen

  D The Statute of Rhuddlan

11 **Where in London is the White Tower?**

  A Tower of London

  B Buckingham Palace

  C Palace of Westminster

  D St Paul's Cathedral

12 **The Scottish Parliament abolished the authority of the Pope in which year?**

  A 1540

  B 1640

  C 1560

  D 1660

13 **How did Jane Seymour die?**

  A Following childbirth

  B She was executed

  C Old age

  D The plague

14 **Who won the English Civil War in 1646?**

  A Parliament

  B The Cavaliers

  C The king

  D None of the above

15 **What special type of windows did many cathedrals built in the Middle Ages have?**

- **A** Arched
- **B** Mullioned
- **C** Stained glass
- **D** Sash

16 **Which of the following statements is correct?**

- **A** Countries are obliged to belong to the Commonwealth.
- **B** Countries join the Commonwealth voluntarily.

17 **Which TWO of the following names may be given to the day before Lent starts?**

- **A** Ash Wednesday
- **B** Shrove Tuesday
- **C** Good Friday
- **D** Pancake Day

18 **Sir Chris Hoy, the famous cyclist, was born in which part of the UK?**

- **A** England
- **B** Scotland
- **C** Isle of Man
- **D** Channel Islands

19 **Which English king led his army to victory at the Battle of Agincourt?**

- **A** Henry V
- **B** Henry VII
- **C** Henry II
- **D** Henry VIII

20 During the 17th century, many people left Britain and Ireland to settle in which of the following places?

- **A** France
- **B** Africa
- **C** America
- **D** London

21 Is the statement below TRUE or FALSE?
It is legal to carry a weapon if it is for self-defence.

- **A** True
- **B** False

22 There was growth in British film, fashion and music during the 1960s. Which TWO of these were very popular sixties British pop groups?

- **A** Abba
- **B** The Beatles
- **C** The Rolling Stones
- **D** The Beach Boys

23 The four shortlisted works for the Turner Prize are shown at which London venue?

- **A** British Museum
- **B** Tate Britain
- **C** National Gallery
- **D** Victoria and Albert Museum

24 Fighting broke out between colonists in North America and British forces in the late 18th century. What did 13 colonies declare in 1776?

- **A** Defeat
- **B** Surrender
- **C** Independence
- **D** An alliance

ANSWERS: PRACTICE TEST 18

			Handbook reference	Study Guide reference
1	D	Chief Constables	145–6	153–4
2	A	True	96	104
3	A	True	56	64
4	B	Equal pay	73	81
5	C	Balthazar's Feast	97–9	105–7
6	C	The Northern Ireland Parliament was suspended and direct rule from the UK was re-introduced.	75	83
7	C	1973	142	150
8	B	Her husband	43	51
9	A	Bulgaria	64–5	72–3
10	D	The Statute of Rhuddlan	35	43
11	A	Tower of London	102–3	110–1
12	C	1560	43	51
13	A	Following childbirth	41	49
14	A	Parliament	46–8	54–6
15	C	Stained glass	37–9	45–7
16	B	Countries join the Commonwealth voluntarily.	141	149
17	B	Shrove Tuesday	88	96
	D	Pancake Day		
18	B	Scotland	92–3	100–1
19	A	Henry V	35	43
20	C	America	52	60
21	B	False	144–5	152–3
22	B	The Beatles	73	81
	C	The Rolling Stones		
23	B	Tate Britain	101	109
24	C	Independence	56	64

PRACTICE TEST 19: WALES

1 Who was Cnut (Canute)?

- **A** A Danish king of England
- **B** An Anglo-Saxon king of England
- **C** A Scottish lord
- **D** A Viking warrior

2 Who is not appointed to the cabinet?

- **A** The Chancellor of the Exchequer
- **B** The Speaker
- **C** The Foreign Secretary
- **D** The Home Secretary

3 Scotland developed its own Parliament. This was divided into three parts. What were they called?

- **A** The lords, the commons and the clergy
- **B** The lords, the commons and the Estates
- **C** The lords, the commons and the Houses
- **D** The lords, the commons and the bishops

4 Is the statement below TRUE or FALSE?
English laws and the English language were introduced to Wales during the Middle Ages.

- **A** True
- **B** False

5 What is the first line of Rudyard Kipling's poem *If*?

- **A** If you can keep your head when all about you
- **B** She walks in beauty, like the night
- **C** What passing-bells for these who die as cattle?
- **D** Oh to be in England now that April's there

6 Looking after the environment involves which TWO of the following?

- **A** Buying new products whenever possible
- **B** Buying recycled products whenever possible
- **C** Recycling waste when possible
- **D** Using more energy when possible

7 It is enshrined in law that men and women in the UK have equal rights to work, own property, marry and which of the following?

- **A** Divorce
- **B** Go to church
- **C** Travel abroad
- **D** Own a dog

8 The Scottish Parliament has how many members?

- **A** 60
- **B** 108
- **C** 129
- **D** 360

9 Who were the Jutes, Angles and Saxons?

- **A** Tribespeople from Northern Europe
- **B** Romans
- **C** Tribespeople from Wales
- **D** Tribespeople from Scotland

10 Which country's coastline did James Cook map, leading to the establishment of a few colonies there?

- **A** Indonesia
- **B** Portugal
- **C** South Africa
- **D** Australia

11 About which conflict did poets Wilfred Owen and Siegfried Sassoon write?

- **A** Crimean War
- **B** Boer War
- **C** First World War
- **D** Second World War

12 What proportion of respondents to the 2009 UK Citizenship Survey identified themselves as Christian?

- **A** 7 out of 10
- **B** 2 out of 10
- **C** 9 out of 10
- **D** 5 out of 10

13 The 'Ashes' are played for between England and Australia in which sport?

- **A** Rugby union
- **B** Tennis
- **C** Darts
- **D** Cricket

14 Emmeline Pankhurst, who was born in Manchester in 1858, had a role in establishing which TWO organisations for women's rights?

- **A** The Women's Voting Council
- **B** The Women's Franchise League
- **C** The Female Democratic Organisation
- **D** The Women's Social and Political Union

15 How are people chosen for a jury?

   A Randomly, from the electoral register

   B Randomly, from the lottery

   C People apply to be on a jury

   D They are appointed by legal professionals

16 Which of these is not famous as a poet?

   A William Wordsworth

   B Alfred Lord Tennyson

   C Percy Shelley

   D Lucian Freud

17 Cowes on the Isle of Wight is most famous in a sporting context for which of the following?

   A Rowing

   B Sailing

   C Fishing championships

   D Surfing

18 Which of the following is not a name for an EU law?

   A Directive

   B Diktat

   C Framework decision

   D Regulation

19 Is the statement below TRUE or FALSE?
The Council of Europe is another name for the European Union.

   A True

   B False

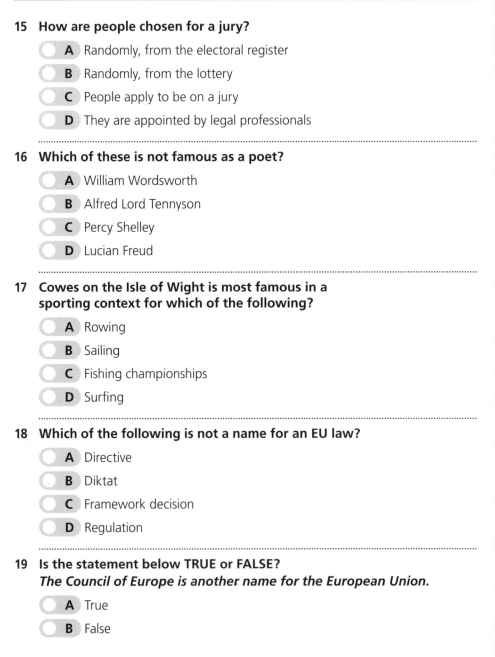

20 What is the reign of Queen Victoria commonly referred to as?

   A The Age of Victoria

   B The Victoria Years

   C The Victorian Age

   D The Victorian Epoch

21 Which of James II's relatives were strictly Protestant?

   A Brothers

   B Sisters

   C Daughters

   D Aunts and uncles

22 You may write to or telephone your MP, or visit him or her where?

   A In the House of Lords

   B At a regular local surgery

   C At Buckingham Palace

   D At his or her London home

23 Pressure and lobby groups represent the interests of which TWO of the following?

   A Minor political parties

   B Foreign ambassadors

   C Business organisations

   D Campaigning organisations

24 At what time is the two-minute silence observed on Remembrance Sunday?

   A 11am

   B Noon

   C 3pm

   D 5pm

ANSWERS: PRACTICE TEST 19

			Handbook reference	Study Guide reference
1	A	A Danish king of England	33	41
2	B	The Speaker	131–2	139–40
3	A	The lords, the commons and the clergy	36–7	44–5
4	A	True	35	43
5	A	If you can keep your head when all about you	63	71
6	B	Buying recycled products whenever possible	164	172
	C	Recycling waste when possible		
7	A	Divorce	83–4	91–2
8	C	129	136	144
9	A	Tribespeople from Northern Europe	31–3	39–41
10	D	Australia	53–5	61–3
11	C	First World War	104–6	112–4
12	A	7 out of 10	84	92
13	D	Cricket	94	102
14	B	The Women's Franchise League	62	70
	D	The Women's Social and Political Union		
15	A	Randomly, from the electoral register	148–9	156–7
16	D	Lucian Freud	101	109
17	B	Sailing	96	104
18	B	Diktat	143	151
19	B	False	143	151
20	C	The Victorian Age	59	67
21	C	Daughters	49	57
22	B	At a regular local surgery	130	138
23	C	Business organisations	132	140
	D	Campaigning organisations		
24	A	11am	90	98

PRACTICE TEST 20

1 **Is the statement below TRUE or FALSE?**
The Scottish Exhibition and Conference Centre is in Edinburgh.

  A True

  B False

2 **Which TWO of the following are famous plays by William Shakespeare?**

  A The Duchess of Malfi

  B Romeo and Juliet

  C A Midsummer Night's Dream

  D Dr Faustus

3 **In which British city is the Royal Crescent?**

  A Bath

  B Exeter

  C Edinburgh

  D Cardiff

4 **During which period of the Christian calendar is it traditional to fast?**

  A Easter

  B Christmas

  C Lent

  D Advent

5 **By the middle of the 15th century, what had happened to the last of the Welsh rebellions?**

  A They had been defeated by the English

  B They had been contained within Wales

  C They were victorious over the English armies

  D They were abandoned because they were too expensive

6   Which British Admiral was killed at the Battle of Trafalgar?

    A Napoleon

    B Nelson

    C Sir Francis Drake

    D Duke of Wellington

7   Which of the following statements is correct?

    A Civil law relates to crimes that are investigated by the police.

    B Civil law relates to disputes between people.

8   Who was responsible for building the Tower of London?

    A William the Conqueror

    B Edward I

    C Henry VIII

    D Elizabeth I

9   Who is the only Briton to have won the Tour de France cycle race?

    A Sir Chris Hoy

    B Sir Bradley Wiggins

    C Mark Cavendish

    D Reg Harris

10   Is it legal to send a girl abroad for circumcision or cutting?

    A Yes, if it is legal in the country to which she is sent

    B No, it is illegal in the UK to send a girl
        abroad for circumcision or cutting

11   Does the Council of Europe have the power to make laws?

    A Yes, but it does not use these powers often

    B No, but it can draft agreements known as conventions and charters

12 **William Beveridge briefly served as an MP and was subsequently leader in the House of Lords for which political party?**

- **A** The Labour Party
- **B** The Liberal Party
- **C** The Conservative Party
- **D** The Green Party

13 **Halloween is regarded historically as which of the following?**

- **A** A Christian festival
- **B** A Muslim festival
- **C** A Pagan festival
- **D** A Sikh festival

14 **Where in Ireland did the English government encourage Scottish and English Protestants to settle during the reigns of Elizabeth I and James I?**

- **A** Ulster
- **B** Dublin
- **C** Cork
- **D** Armagh

15 **A famous boat race for rowers is contested on the River Thames each year between which TWO university teams?**

- **A** Cambridge and London
- **B** Edinburgh and Oxford
- **C** Edinburgh and London
- **D** Cambridge and Oxford

16 **Penicillin was developed into a usable drug by Howard Florey and which other scientist?**

- **A** Stephen Hawking
- **B** Marie Curie
- **C** Albert Einstein
- **D** Ernst Chain

17 **Which artist, born in 1937, is famous for his contribution to the 'pop art' movement of the 1960s?**

- **A** Lucian Freud
- **B** John Petts
- **C** David Hockney
- **D** Robert Lenkiewicz

18 **Members of the Northern Ireland Assembly have worked together successfully since which year?**

- **A** 2000
- **B** 2003
- **C** 2007
- **D** 2011

19 **Which of these is not a UK regional language?**

- **A** Welsh
- **B** Irish Gaelic
- **C** Gaelic
- **D** Kentish

20 Which of the statements below is not correct?

- **A** More women than men study at university.
- **B** There are now more female MPs than male MPs.
- **C** Employment opportunities for women are much greater than they were in the past.
- **D** Women work in all sectors of the economy.

21 Ellie Simmonds is a Paralympic gold medallist in which sport?

- **A** Archery
- **B** Athletics
- **C** Swimming
- **D** Table tennis

22 Is the statement below TRUE or FALSE?
Hospitals often need donated blood to help people who are ill or injured.

- **A** True
- **B** False

23 In the Church of Scotland, who is the Moderator?

- **A** A key figure who is responsible for all relations with the Church of England
- **B** A financial overseer who has overall responsibility for the accounts of the Church
- **C** The spiritual leader of the Church, who is appointed for life
- **D** The chairperson of the General Assembly, who is appointed for one year only and often speaks on behalf of the Church

24 Which of the following statements is correct?

- **A** Mary, Queen of Scots hoped Elizabeth I might help her regain her throne.
- **B** Mary, Queen of Scots had no faith that Elizabeth I might help her.

ANSWERS: PRACTICE TEST 20

			Handbook reference	Study Guide reference
1	B	False	97–9	105–7
2	B	Romeo and Juliet	34	52
	C	A Midsummer Night's Dream		
3	A	Bath	102–3	110–1
4	C	Lent	88	96
5	A	They had been defeated by the English	35	43
6	B	Nelson	56–7	64–5
7	B	Civil law relates to disputes between people.	144–5	152–3
8	A	William the Conqueror	120	128
9	B	Sir Bradley Wiggins	92–3	100–1
10	B	No, it is illegal in the UK to send a girl abroad for circumcision or cutting	155	163
11	B	No, but it can draft agreements known as conventions and charters	143	151
12	B	The Liberal Party	71	79
13	C	A Pagan festival	90	98
14	A	Ulster	45	53
15	D	Cambridge and Oxford	96	104
16	D	Ernst Chain	70	78
17	C	David Hockney	101	109
18	C	2007	133–7	141–5
19	D	Kentish	82	90
20	B	There are now more female MPs than male MPs.	83–4	91–2
21	C	Swimming	92–3	100–1
22	A	True	162	170
23	D	The chairperson of the General Assembly, who is appointed for one year only and often speaks on behalf of the Church	85	93
24	A	Mary, Queen of Scots hoped Elizabeth I might help her regain her throne.	43	51